Princeton Theological

Dikran Y. Hadidian

General Editor

14

SEARCHING FOR LOST COINS
Explorations in Christianity and Feminism

Searching for Lost Coins

*Explorations in Christianity
and Feminism*

ANN LOADES

PICKWICK PUBLICATIONS
Allison Park, Pennsylvania

First published in Great Britain 1987
SPCK
Holy Trinity Church
Marylebone Road
London NW1 4DU

And in the United States of America in 1988 by
Pickwick Publications
4137 Timberlane Drive
Allison Park, Pennsylvania 15101

Library of Congress Cataloging-in-Publication Data

Loades, Ann
    Searching for lost coins.

    (Princeton theological monograph series ; 14)
    Bibliography: p.
    1. Women in Christianity. 2. Feminism--Religious
aspects--Christianity. I. Title. II. Series.
BV639.W7L54 1988   261.8'344   88-1056
ISBN 1-55635-000-7

CONTENTS

v

ACKNOWLEDGEMENTS

Some of the material of chapter 3 appeared originally in *Images of Belief in Literature*, ed. by David Jasper (Macmillan 1984) and in *Religion and Literature* (17, 2, 1985).

The poetry of Emily Dickinson is reprinted by permission of the publishers and the Trustees of Amherst College from *The Poems of Emily Dickinson*, ed. by Thomas H. Johnson (Cambridge, Mass., The Belknap Press of Harvard University Press, Copyright 1951, © 1955, 1979, 1983 by the President and Fellows of Harvard College).

Material from the *Notebooks* of Simone Weil, trans. by A. Wills, is by permission of Routledge & Kegan Paul Plc; the quotation on pp. 91–2 is by permission of Joan Chamberlain Engelsman; that on p. 93 is by permission of Penguin Books.

The quotation on p. 24 from Helen Waddell's *The Wandering Scholars* is by permission of Constable & Co. Ltd. and by A. P. Watt; the quotations on pp. 23–4, p. 25, and on pp. 28–9 from Helen Waddell's *More Latin Lyrics* are by permission of Miss Mary M. Martin.

The translation of Paul Claudel's poem on p. 51 is by permission of Professor K. O'Flaherty and Cork University Press.

The quotation from 'A Vision: Thinking of Simone Weil' by Adrienne Rich on p. 47 is by permission of Adrienne Rich and W. W. Norton & Co.

The quotations from 'Lady Lazarus' and *Three Women* by Sylvia Plath on pp. 49–50 and p. 89 are by permission of Olwyn Hughes.

PREFACE

The five papers in this book were written in response to an invitation which came to me from the Scott Holland Trust to give some lectures on 'theology and the significance of gender'. The 'Holland Lectureship' was founded in 1920 'for the purpose of a Memorial' to perpetuate the 'memory and influence' of Henry Scott Holland, Regius Professor of Divinity in the University of Oxford, Canon of Christ Church, Oxford, and formerly Canon of St Paul's, London. The focus of the Lectures is to be 'the religion of the Incarnation in its bearing on the social and economic life of man'.

My five lectures (and a seminar) were delivered as Public Lectures in the University of Newcastle on Tyne, and I remain very grateful to the University for extending its hospitality to me in this way. My thanks especially to the Scott Holland Trust for the invitation; to the Rt Revd Kenneth Woollcombe, Chairman of the Trust, who chaired my first lecture; and to Professor John Sawyer of the Department of Religious Studies, University of Newcastle on Tyne, who made it possible for me to give the lectures there (and the seminar in his department), and who chaired the fifth lecture.

I received much kindness and support from my other 'chairs': Dr Cecily Boulding OP, of Ushaw College, Durham; Mrs Mary Midgley and Mrs Judith Hughes, both of Newcastle University; as well as from my friends, notably Mrs Linda Fenton and Canon John Fenton, Dr Jane Wheare and Dr Michael Banner, Dr Richard Roberts, Mrs Alison Jasper and Dr David Jasper, Professor A. O. Dyson, Dss (now Deacon) Juliet Woollcombe, Mrs Joy Sykes and Professor S. W. Sykes, Mrs Patricia Vereker and Professor C. H. Vereker, Dom Columba Stewart of St John's Abbey, Minnesota, and Dom Alberic Stacpoole of St Benet's Hall, Oxford. To none of these should be attributed the opinions expressed in the lectures, the responsibility for which remains my own.

Special thanks also go to Professor W. A. Whitehouse, and to

ix

Mr John Lowe, Director of Studies at Ushaw College, both of whom made pertinent comments on the original typescript of the lectures; and to Mrs Margaret Parkinson, of Durham University Theology Department, who produced the final typescript. Miss Isobel Wollaston was invaluable in drafting the bibliography for me.

I learned much from my audiences both in Newcastle and in St Peter's College, Oxford; Christ Church, Oxford; the Ecumenical Society of the Blessed Virgin Mary (Oxford Branch); the Hort Society, Cambridge; Durham University Lightfoot Society; Sheffield Theological Society; Ushaw College, Durham; and at Rhodes College, Memphis, Tennessee; and I am grateful for many casual conversations with friends and acquaintances too numerous to name.

March 1987 ANN LOADES

1

SEARCHING FOR LOST COINS

Reform and reformers in a patriarchal society

The Scott Holland Trust proposed to me as the topic for my lectures, 'Theology and the Significance of Gender'. I believe that the Trust did so because that topic lies at the very heart of the debate about the relationship between the two complex phenomena of 'Christianity' and 'feminism'. By 'gender' I mean what any particular society makes of the biological differences which make some of us women and some of us men. Theology is itself a gender-related term for our naming and talking about divine reality, and we need to be critically aware, perhaps most of all in worship, that God is not anthropomorphically merely masculine (theology) and cannot be anthropomorphically merely feminine (thealogy) either. We can no longer avoid gender issues in theology, however controversial the empirical study of gender may be within its appropriate research fields, with gender issues polarizing social scientists, for instance, no less than theologians. Gender as an aid to analysis helps us to examine the way in which our religious traditions work, the symbolism which they use, the characteristics of roles within them, and the way in which religious traditions both reflect social assumptions and shape and reshape those assumptions. Much of what I offer in the first four chapters is about roles, social assumptions and symbolism, and I attempt to address myself directly to theology/thealogy and the significance of gender in the last chapter.

My concern at this stage of my own initial engagement with the problems of the relationship between Christianity and feminism is with those still inclined to be interested in the fate of Christianity, rather than with forms of post-Christian feminism (often still a religious form of feminism). Dr Daphne Hampson of the University of St Andrews is its main exponent in the United Kingdom. Nor am I in any way competent to do more than acknowledge the importance of inter-religious feminist dialogue which is the province of Dr Ursula King of the University of Leeds. I write, therefore, with the working assumption that Christianity may still make a contribution to the perceptions of

1

those concerned to try to shape new futures for women and men and the relationships which may obtain between them. I take it that feminism is here to stay, since the agenda of seeking justice for women arises from 'serious troubles affecting the lives of large numbers of ordinary people', though Mary Midgley and Judith Hughes, the writers of that remark in *Women's Choices*, go on to add that feminism needs to be put 'in the context of a full set of ideals and a fair programme of other humane enterprises'.[1]

If 'Christian feminism' is not a contradiction in terms, what I think it may represent is the conviction that distinctively Christian faith may help to renovate a sense of human community, coinherence even, between women and men, assuming of course that most human communities will continue to include both sexes, still on the whole able to celebrate each other's company, and able to explore reality together without the enchantment of the over-simplification that attributes all our problems to the male of the human species. Whatever else Christianity may be about, it includes hope of change for the better in response to divinely experienced grace, and in particular it is meant to embody justice between those deemed to be enemies, even those venomously labelled as 'gangrenous patriarchs'—an abusive response to the nastiness of 'castrating bitch'. Such justice, the fruit of which could be reconciliation without domination, should be the expression of the diaconate, the service rendered to society by Christianity.[2] It is put with astonishing generosity in the diaries of Etty Hillesum, a twenty-eight-year-old Dutch woman of Jewish descent, who wrote on 23 September 1942, not long before her final deportation to the extermination camp in which she died on 30 November 1943, 'It is the only thing we can do ... I see no alternative, each of us must turn inwards and destroy in himself all that he thinks he ought to destroy in others. And remember that every atom of hate we add to this world makes it still more inhospitable'. Her friend replies '... that is nothing but Christianity!' to which she responds, 'and why ever not?'[3]

My last preliminary comment is that I have discovered that the argument which Christian feminists have with their own religious tradition is in so many respects provided for women by Christianity itself. To learn about this is, to steal an analogy from Dorothy Sayers, like watching someone engaged in the process of trying to force a large and obstreperous cat (which we shall deem to be female) into a small basket.

> As fast as you tuck in the head, the tail comes out, when you have at last confined the hind legs, the fore-paws come out and scratch; and when, after a painful struggle, you shut down the lid, the dismal wailings of the imprisoned animal suggest that some essential dignity in the creature has been violated and a wrong done to its very nature.[4]

So then to Henry Scott Holland, the author of 'Judge eternal, throned in splendour', a hymn by which one can capture something of his spirit without reading through his lectures and sermons!

Searching for lost coins is one feminine-related term for 'the relentless, almost obsessive quest of the Creator for the creature'.[5] It can be used nowadays for women's hunt for their history, but Henry Scott Holland used it to express what he called 'social fellowship': 'The single sheep out on the hills belongs already to the fold; therefore it is that the search is so unflagging... This is what contributes to the joy of the recovery, that the hundredth is brought back again to the ninety-nine, the lost piece to the nine that are waiting for their completion'. And the prodigal in the far country comes to himself 'when he flings over his detached and separate self and regards himself as belonging to a household and a city'.[6] In his concern for 'social fellowship', he was acutely sensitive to the problems that women faced in his lifetime. This, in my view, corresponds with the period which helped to precipitate the most recent phase of the argument that women have with Christianity. Writing in 1911 when he was sixty-four, he knew that in asking 'What is man?' that he was asking, also, 'What is true womanhood?':

> And what is its place, and function, and work, and claim? That is the crucial problem that we must, at all costs, face and solve. We dare not put it off a moment longer. The issue is laid upon us, whether we will or no. We have laid hold of women in masses, and put them to industrial use. They have been swept into our social grind. They are hard at it. They share our heaviest burdens. They feel the horrible pressure of our ruthless mechanism more than any. They are most liable of all to be crushed under the wheels and driven to the wall. They are broken: they are pushed over into sin: hell gapes for them. The situation can bear the strain no longer. We have got to consider it afresh from the beginning. We have got to secure for women an entirely new value and significance.

3

He seems to have doubted whether this could be done equitably and surely, until 'women themselves are allowed to have their say in determining what that value shall be, and in declaiming that significance':

> Will the due consideration, which their case so urgently demands, ever be given until they can have some power to enforce it? Many of us think that the dead-weight of indifference will never be lifted while men alone are left to take the decisive step. The women who know, in the bitterness of their souls, what the stress signifies and all the terror of the perils to which their weakness is exposed, will bring to bear upon the situation the force of passion and conviction which will remove the obstructions and compel a settlement.

He wrote in this way before the fight for the vote had been won, but he foresaw that the legislation of the future would deal with matters with which women were intimately and vitally concerned. He thought it a matter of Christian responsibility and citizenship to secure that what was done was after the mind 'of Him whom women alone companioned to the last, and believed in to the uttermost, and laid in His tomb, with the spices of their unconquerable faithfulness and love: of Him whom a woman first saw as He rose, and spoke His first word on His Resurrection morning to a woman... '[7] It was those same women who were sent back 'with a message of hope, of activity, of life, from the tomb itself ... women who must drop their spices and myrrh, and go back to urgent business, to rouse faint-hearted men, to bid them believe, and rise and act, and go to Galilee, and obey and hope'.[8] It could well be said that this need to secure for women a new evaluation represented one of the most important of the contemporary challenges to faith of which he wrote in *Lux Mundi* (1889), one of those 'thirsts that it had not prepared itself to satisfy'.[9]

Women in western industrialized culture had become clearer about what their wrongs were during Scott Holland's lifetime, and it was their political campaigns which helped to give their argument with Christian institutions its sharp cutting edge. It is the political context which continues to shape North American feminist theology—so widely read over here—quite explicitly. In an essay published in a new collection edited by Letty Russell,[10] Elisabeth Schüssler Fiorenza writes of the authorization that the Bible, the foundation document of Christianity, has provided for

4

women who rejected slavery, colonial exploitation and anti-Semitism as well as misogynism (hatred of women). But she writes this *after* saying:

> From its inception, feminist interpretation and concern with Scripture has been generated by the fact that the Bible was used to halt the emancipation of women and slaves. Not only in the last century but also today, the political Right laces its attacks against the feminist struggle for women's rights and freedoms in the political, economic, reproductive, intellectual and religious spheres with biblical quotations and appeals to scriptural authority. From countless pulpits and Sunday School classes, such patriarchal attacks are proclaimed as the 'word of God'. Anti-ERA groups, the cultural Total Woman movement, and the Moral Majority appeal to the teachings of the Bible on the American family and on creational differences between the sexes resulting in a different societal and ecclesial calling. At the same time, the political Right does not hesitate to quote the Bible against shelters for battered women, for physical punishment of children, against abortion even in cases of rape or child pregnancy, and against women's studies programmes at state universities.[11]

It is an interesting miscellany, but even without trying to engage in what would no doubt be an instructive exercise,—rewriting that paragraph with specific reference to the British situation—one can appreciate why she wants to place a warning on all biblical texts: *'Caution! Could be dangerous to your health and survival!'* This it seems to me had become absolutely clear during the last century as never perhaps before, when the Bible had an authority which, in Britain, it is unlikely to recover in the foreseeable future. We know now how painful it can be to assimilate the critical discussion of the biblical texts, but better to live with that pain than to return to the nineteenth century and the period when a very few women were only just beginning, along with some men, to learn about modern criticism, and the sensitivity of that criticism to the dynamics of the biblical texts and their relationship to what else surrounds them.

During Scott Holland's lifetime there had been extraordinary gains and improvements to the lot of women, even though there was still a long way to go in conceding them, for example, not only the exercise of their rationality in the power to vote, but in contributing to their religious traditions in new ways. As Mary Midgley has recently written:

Both actual women and their symbolism were expected to remain outside the blaze of cerebral daylight. It was taken for granted that emotion would not actually lose its influence, because women would still supply it. Families would still be kept going. And the inconvenience caused by collisions between so many hard, resistant, autonomous individuals would be kept within bounds, because the customary cushions would still abound. Hinc illae lacrimae. Hence, that is, the alarm and horror which arose whenever it was suggested that women too might have an intellect and a will... [12]

The fate of the cushions was to continue to be under debate, but what then had been the gains? When Scott Holland was born in 1847, ten years before the Matrimonial Causes Act of 1857[13] and its development in legislation of 1867 and 1870, a *married* woman — and marriage in Protestant cultures was the likely destination of many, as of course were periods of widowhood—a married woman had no legal existence, and no legal rights of property ownership. Everything that she owned, earned or inherited belonged to her husband, unless her family were rich enough to give her some financial protection via her marriage settlements. This is, to say the least of it, interesting in a society in which those contracting legally valid marriages did so in accordance with the Established Church's 1662 Prayer Book, which contained the husband's affirmation that *he* would endow his wife with all *his* worldly goods. Barbara Taylor has drawn attention to the analogy with slavery, for the double moral standard in sexuality was also legally entrenched: an adulterous wife lost all her rights to maintenance and could be abandoned on the basis of a judicial separation; an adulterous husband suffered no penalty, but could pursue a wife, who left him on account of his infidelity, and sue those who gave her shelter. If he abandoned her, he could be made to provide support only on the basis of a court order establishing her need. He could beat her so long as the stick was no thicker than a man's thumb. [14]

A woman had not been able to determine where her children lived, or how they were to be educated. If her husband died, guardianship passed to her nearest male relative. Since it cost over £1,000 to get a Private Members Bill through Parliament, she had few divorce opportunities, unless her rich husband chose to initiate them, and if divorced or separated from her husband, no rights either to keep or have access to her children. It was Caroline Norton's campaigns, through friends acting on her behalf, to get this changed, which led to the situation where a wife deserted by her husband could keep her earnings, receive separate maintenance, inherit and bequeath property, could sue, be sued, and make contracts—have in fact the rights of unmarried women. Not until 1885 when Scott Holland was thirty-five, did the Married Woman's Property Act secure to married women the property and earnings they had acquired after marriage.

Yet it could be held, as Caroline Norton had seen, that once a young woman had made a choice to marry, 'the boundaries of duty, religion and social necessity are walls round a woman's heart and light fences round a man's'.[15] For she, after all, promised to obey him in marriage, that essential indicator of apparently 'biblically' based subordination and submission, which rests on the misinterpretation of Ephesians 5.[16] An elderly woman in 1834 wrote in *The Pioneer* how, if a woman offered the least resistance to her husband, that resistance could be thrust back down her throat with his fist, possibly with the loss of a tooth or a spilling of a little of that blood which he thought so inferior to his own. 'As he is lord of the castle, he is master and must be obeyed.'[17] No wonder that the association of woman's lot with slavery was so powerful; and a recent paper by Susan Brooks Thistlethwaite[18] documents how in the USA at least, women can still believe that they are inferior in status before husband and God and somehow deserve a life of pain, given the peculiar connection in the Christian tradition of women's lives with depravity. One woman says simply, 'God punished women more'. Religious beliefs, then as now, can reinforce passivity in the face of verbal and physical abuse, not least when marriage is seen as a kind of representation of the divine-human relationship, that is in turn understood as one of domination and submission-to-be-expressed-by-women, but not by men.

The rejection of this passivity can be seen with absolute clarity in Mary Chavelita Dunne's short story 'Virgin Soil', one of her collection of stories known as *Keynotes and Discords*, which were first published in 1893-4 under her pen-name of George Egerton, and recently republished by Virago.[19] Having left her adulterous husband, the young woman in the story returns home, aged twenty-two, to have it out with her mother, who had married her off at seventeen in as total ignorance of her own sexuality as of that of her husband:

> You gave me to a man, nay more, you told me to obey him, to believe that whatever he said would be right, would be my duty; knowing that the meaning of marriage was a sealed book to me, that I had no real idea of what union with a man meant. You delivered me body and soul into his hands without preparing me in any way for the ordeal I was to go through. You sold me for a home, for clothes, for food; you played upon my ignorance, I won't say innocence, that is different.[20]

In these circumstances, 'a man demands from his wife as a right, what he must sue from a mistress as a favour', and marriage became for many women 'a legal prostitution, a nightly degradation, a hateful yoke under which they age, mere bearers of children conceived in a sense of duty, not love'. Granted that some began their marriages with love, 'the mystery, the crowning glory of their lives, is turned into a duty they submit to with distaste instead of a favour granted to a husband, who must become a new lover to obtain it'. Her mother says desperately at this point, 'But men are different ... you can't refuse a husband, you might cause him to commit sin', to which the daughter replies, 'Bosh, mother, he is responsible for his own sins, we are not bound to dry-nurse his morality. Man is what we have made him, his very faults are of our making. No wife is bound to set aside the demands of her individual soul for the sake of imbecile obedience.'[21]

No wonder then, that Eliza Sharples had addressed a meeting in 1832 in these terms:

> The tyrant God, Necessity, said to the subject man: 'Of the tree of the knowledge of good and evil thou shalt not eat'. Sweet and fair liberty stepped in ... spurned the order ... of the tyrant, 'She took of the fruit thereof, and did eat, and gave also to her husband with her, and he did eat.' Do you not, with one voice exclaim, well done woman! LIBERTY FOR EVER! If that was a fall, sirs, it was a glorious fall, and such a fall as is now wanted ... I will be such an Eve, so bright a picture of Liberty![22]

Some ten years later, in 1844, the reformer Emma Martin, who once lectured on 'The Holy Ghost, HER Nature, Offices and Laws', tartly reported that: 'I have asked the *learned* (?) clergy for rational answers to knotty questions ... they wont [sic] answer them because they are asked by a *woman*, yet they obtain Christ from the same source. I wonder they did not object to *him* on that account'.[23]

Liberty then was crucially connected to the development of rationality, and so education for girls and women was essential to reform. Emily Davies's campaigns arose in part out of her sojourn in a Gateshead vicarage, to which she came, aged ten, with her family in 1840, and where a school run by one of her father's curates was, at her father's request, restricted to boys, on the grounds that the presence of girls would lower its status. Twenty years later in London she was to reply to worries about 'brain-fever' in over-pressed female intellects with the question, 'Why should simple equations brighten their intellects and quadratic equations drive them into a lunatic asylum?'[24] She and Florence Nightingale, (amongst others) began to tackle the parasite status of some women—the association of femininity with indolence—when it was so transparently evident that many others were experiencing in their lives anything but the idealization of women and of their maternalism, an idealism that may have been a reaction to the opposing trend of women entering paid work in ever greater numbers.

One very useful text which helped women and men to understand how it was that women had come to accept idealization via narcissism was Olive Schreiner's *The Story of an African Farm* (1883),[25] the work of a young woman who had been brought up in a biblically-soaked culture and who, in 1875, had begun to work on her novel in isolation—at about the age of twenty, a novel which was a major publishing success in Britain. I mention from that novel first Olive Schreiner's comparison of the way in which a woman's life comes to fit her:

> We fit our sphere as a Chinese woman's foot fits her shoe, exactly, as though God had made both—and yet He knows nothing of either. In some of us the shaping to our end has been quite completed. The parts we are not to use have been quite atrophied, and have even dropped off; but in others, and we are not less to be pitied, they have been weakened and left. We wear the bandages, but our limbs have not grown to them; we know that we are compressed, and chafe against them.
>
> But what does it help? A little bitterness, a little longing when we are young, a little futile searching for work, a little passionate striving for room for the exercise of our powers—and then we go with the drove. A woman must march with her regiment. In the end she must be trodden down or go with it; and if she is wise she goes.[26]

9

This to a reader of modern feminist literature recalls evidence of the subordination of women in non-Christian culture, and Mary Daly's gruesome analysis of suttee, genital mutilation, witch-burning, arguably some recent gynaecological practices, as well as footbinding.[27]

Olive Schreiner's novel was sometimes burned and removed from the shelves of circulating libraries because of its analysis of the parasite status of the 'ideal' woman, and the narcissism that they learned (Lyndall indeed dies gazing at herself in a mirror that she holds up to her face), as well of course because its heroine did not marry, nor did she live happily ever after. She died soon after giving birth to a child who had died. Yet this novel survived because it articulated for so many women what they had felt, but had been unable to say.[28] Together with Ibsen's *The Doll's House*,[29] the novel had begun to force on men the problems of the women whose gender they had helped to construct as parasites or dolls—without yet having to come to terms with the facts of the labour of the women engaged in the paid or unpaid labour force. This was a subject that Olive Schreiner was to tackle in one of her later writings, *Women and Labour* (1911), rewritten during the Boer war as the British call it, when she was virtually under house-arrest for her opposition to the war. Indeed in her writing we can find some of the argument which has continued to associate central elements of the feminist critique of our culture with pacifism. Looking at death on South African battlefields she wrote: 'We pay the first cost on all human life... No woman who is a woman says of a human body, "It is nothing!"'[30] She was alert to the importance of women's being able to exercise the vote as a sign of their rationality, leaving the Cape Colony Enfranchisement League because the League would not commit itself to the fight for votes for *all* the women of Cape Colony and not just the white women.[31]

In *The Story of an African Farm* Lyndall remained a passionate optimist about the future for women, though this was a hope without possibility of achievement for her in her isolation. She knew the obstacles in her way. 'When we ask to be doctors, lawyers, law-makers, anything but ill-paid drudges, they say, — No; but you have men's chivalrous attention; now think of that and be satisfied! What would you do without it?'[32] And to Waldo, 'We are not to study law, nor science, nor art; so we study you.

There is never a nerve or fibre in your man's nature but we know it.'[33] She wanted to be born in the future, when to be born a woman would not be to be born branded: 'A great soul draws and is drawn with a more fierce intensity than any small one. By every inch we grow in intellectual height our love strikes down its roots deeper, and spreads out its arms wider. It is for love's sake yet more than for any other that we look for that new time.' Love is not for buying or selling, not a means of making bread, but the result of the time when a woman's life would be filled with earnest, independent labour, but of herself, all that she could say was that 'To see the good and the beautiful... and to have no strength to live it, is only to be Moses on the mountain of Nebo, with the land at your feet and no power to enter. It would be better not to see it.'[34] Eventually in the bitterness of her tears she found that 'The lifting up of the hands brings no salvation; redemption is from within, and neither from God nor man; it is wrought out by the soul itself, with suffering and through time.'[35] When Olive Schreiner visited England to find herself celebrated for this novel, she found what 'Lyndall' had needed in her desperation, which was the opportunity to combine with others to bring about change.

I want, finally, in this chapter to turn to mention two more reformers and draw attention to the critical text on the Bible which emerged in the last century, Elizabeth Cady Stanton's *The Woman's Bible* of 1895 and 1898. The two reformers can be connected. The first reformer is Josephine Butler,[36] born into the Northumbrian family which produced Earl Grey of Reform fame, and a family in which she received an education as good as that of her brothers. She was to marry most blessedly an equally remarkable man, whom she met when he was a tutor at University College, Durham. He was to become a Canon of Winchester, and with her three sons, and her two brothers-in-law, he stood absolutely rock solid behind her campaigns for the repeal of the Contagious Diseases Acts of 1864–9 (finally repealed in 1886), which meant that *any* woman suspected of being a prostitute could be forced to undergo a vaginal examination at a police station. Josephine Butler had discovered the connections between seduction, abandonment, low wages, starvation and prostitution; and anger at this legislation, aimed at women rather than at the *army* which the legislation was supposed to protect,

11

precipitated her into the first of her major campaigns.

Her anger, and the pain she suffered at the tragic death of her small daughter in an accident at home, pushed her into her next assault, on the double standard of morality, with W. H. Stead, a former editor of the *Northern Echo* in Darlington, who became editor of the *Pall Mall Gazette*. They investigated 'West End' prostitution, and in their July 1885 edition of the *Pall Mall Gazette* they published 'The maiden tribute of modern Babylon', a description of the circumstances in which children became prostitutes—not perhaps quite identical with those obtaining today. Zena Fay Pierce in the USA made an apt remark when she said that 'Bad morals will exist only as long as virtuous women do not choose to look at all they see, to understand all they hear, and to tell all they know.'[37]

Scott Holland himself saw Josephine Butler at the height of her campaign with Stead:

> She was passing through her martyrdom. The splendid beauty of her face, so spiritual in its high and clear outlines, bore the mark of that death upon it to which she stood daily and hourly committed. There was no hell on earth into which she would not willingly travel, if, by sacrifice of herself, she could reach a hand of help to those poor children whom nothing short of such sacrifice could touch.
>
>   *   *   *
>
> She was driven on and on, along the way of her Calvary, by the poignant memory of her own child, in her beauty and grace, swept out of her arms into the night. It is the children, the girl-children, whom she must spend herself to save.[38]

Elizabeth Cady Stanton heard Josephine Butler campaigning on one of her visits to England in 1882, and Josephine Butler's courage is recalled in the commentary on Numbers 31.9-18, 28-35 in *The Woman's Bible*, a work which she published when she was eighty, and which ran through seven printings in six months and was in 1985 republished in a British edition.[39] Elizabeth Cady Stanton was a veteran of the anti-slavery campaign as well as of challenges to some notorious legal trials. She had turned her attention more particularly to women's rights after her experiences at the meeting of the Anti-Slavery campaign on 12 June, 1840 in London. At this meeting women delegates and guests were seated in a railed-off space at one side of the floor, and were allowed to remain only for the business meetings. A story that she told in 1877 about herself is instructive too. She had, as a seventeen-year old, joined a church auxiliary to finance the education of a young minister. The women sewed, baked, brewed and stewed, held fairs and 'sociables', etc. When the young man graduated, they bought him a black broadcloth suit, a high hat and a cane and invited him to preach. And he chose as his text the line from 1 Timothy, 'I suffer not a woman to speak in church'. She and the other young women walked out, thus one might say constituting themselves the forerunners of the women who heard Mary Daly's 'Exodus' sermon of 14 November, 1971 in Harvard[40]—the first time a woman had preached at a Sunday service in its three hundred and thirty-six years of history. At the conclusion of the sermon the preacher herself led the walk-out from the chapel. No wonder then that Elizabeth Cady Stanton referred to the pulpit as the coward's castle,[41] from which she had heard nothing to rouse women from the apathy of ages, to inspire them to do and to dare great things, to intellectual and spiritual achievements.

In her experience, it had been from the pulpit, when there were biblical models like Deborah and Miriam and Huldah available, that women were given lessons in meekness and self-abnegation, and ever with covered heads as their badge of servitude, were told that they were unfit to sit as delegates to church conferences, to be ordained, to fill the offices of elder, deacon or trustee, or to enter the Holy of Holies in cathedrals.[42] She was acute too about the amalgam of canon and civil law, church and state, priests and legislators, political parties and religious denominations which had all alike taught women's inferiority.

Women in the USA had been badly let down in 1868 when after they had helped to win the anti-slavery campaign, they were nonetheless excluded from citizenship rights—a wrong only corrected in the USA in 1919. Mary Church Terrell in 1912 was to write that:

> The founders of this republic called heaven and earth to witness that it should be called a government of the people, for the people and by the people; and yet the elective franchise is withheld from one-half of its citizens, many of whom are intelligent, virtuous and cultured, and unstintingly bestowed upon the other half, many of whom are illiterate, degraded and vicious, because by an unparalleled exhibition of lexicographical acrobatics, the word 'people' has been turned to

13

mean all who were shrewd and wise enough to have themselves born boys instead of girls and white instead of black. [43]

Non-inclusive language had therefore also been rumbled, and Elizabeth Cady Stanton came to insist precisely on that self-reliance of women in understanding themselves so characteristic of twentieth-century feminism, not least in biblical interpretation. She takes us into the present-day agenda and to the discovery of new ways of interpreting some of the biblical texts, which had been supposed to authorize women's subordination. [44] I refer here particularly to Phyllis Trible's claim for the development of biblical theology as women's work, [45] and for the movement in feminist theology which argues quite rightly, in my view, that centuries of certain habits of exegesis now stand under judgement, as do the biblical texts themselves—and all without immunity.

We may well then appreciate anew the text from Revelation 3.8, which captured the imagination of the 1920 North Carolina Conference of the Women's Missionary Society: 'Behold, I have set before thee an open door, and no man can shut it.'[46] It is worth recalling the support for women which was being expressed in some interesting and non-theological ways too, and thus helping to shape the minds and hearts of later generations, such as those who came to read Forster's *A Room with a View* of 1908 (in the course of disposing of the unspeakable Cecil and his deplorable habit of feeling that he must lead women, though he knew not whither, and protect them, though he knew not against what). A woman by Forster's time had

> marked the kingdom of this world, how full it is of wealth, and beauty and war—a radiant crust, built around the central fires, spinning towards the receding heavens. Men, declaring that she inspired them to it, move joyfully over the surface, having the most delightful meetings with other men, happy, not because they are masculine, but because they are alive. Before the show breaks up she would like to drop the august title of the Eternal Woman, and go there as her transitory self.[47]

In this introductory chapter I have attempted to pick out some of the features of feminism in its connections with Christianity and show how they helped to trigger off a variety of twentieth-century concerns. In the following three chapters I will turn back beyond the nineteenth century to some of the features of the Christian tradition which make it such a paradoxical resource for us today. In each case, I try to relate the past to the present via the writings of twentieth-century women, in particular Dorothy Sayers, Helen Waddell, Simone Weil and Virginia Woolf. It will quickly become evident that I do not conceive resources for theological reflection in too narrow terms. I hope that the variety of illustration that I use will be helpful and shift the discussion into fresh areas for discussion and debate. In the final chapter I look at 'theology and the significance of gender' especially, and offer a final concluding comment. I make no apologies for appearing to be polemical in what I write, as I can only engage with the material I have studied in a way that provokes me to see how serious is the debate between Christianity and feminism, and take the risk that for myself, as for others, to profess Christianity in one way or another may become increasingly impossible as a result.

Notes

1 Mary Midgley and Judith Hughes, *Women's Choices: Philosophical Problems facing Feminism* (Weidenfeld and Nicholson 1983), p. 219

2 W. A. Whitehouse, 'Christological Understanding' in *The Authority of Grace* (T. and T. Clark 1981), pp. 99–110.

3 *An Interrupted Life: the Diaries of Etty Hillesum, 1941–1943* (New York, Pocket Books, 1985) pp. 22–3.

4 Dorothy Sayers, 'Creative mind' [on the quarrel of words between the sciences and the humanities], *Unpopular Opinions* (Gollancz 1946), pp. 43–4.

5 D. M. MacKinnon, *Explorations in Theology*, 5 (SCM Press 1979), p. 169.

6 Henry Scott Holland, 'The Household of Faith' *Fibres of Faith* (Wells, Gardner, Darton and Co. 1910), p. 110.

7 Henry Scott Holland, 'What is Man?' in *Our Neighbours: A Handbook for the C.S.U.* (Mowbray 1911), pp. 131–42, esp. pp. 141–2. See also B. M. G. Reardon (ed.), *Henry Scott Holland: A Selection from his Writings* (SPCK 1962).

8 Stephen Paget (ed.), *Henry Scott Holland: Memoir and Letters* (Murray 1921), p. 293.

9 Charles Gore (ed.), *Lux Mundi: A Series of Studies in the Religion of the Incarnation* (Murray 1904), p. 2.

Searching for Lost Coins

10   Letty M. Russell (ed.), *Feminist Interpretation of the Bible* (Basil Blackwell 1985).

11   Elisabeth Schüssler Fiorenza, 'The Will to Choose or to Reject: Continuing our Critical Work' in Russell, op. cit., pp. 125–36, esp. p. 129.

12   Mary Midgley, 'Sex and Personal Identity' (*Encounter*, June 1984), p. 54.

13   Margaret Forster, *Significant Sisters: the Grass Roots of Active Feminism, 1839–1939* (Penguin 1984); see esp. her chapter on Caroline Norton, 1808–77.

14   Barbara Taylor, *Eve and the New Jerusalem: Socialism and Feminism in the Nineteenth Century* (Virago 1984), p. 35.

15   Forster, *Significant Sisters*, p. 49.

16   Dr John McHugh, in 'Una Caro: The Biblical Theme and its Place in the New Covenant', an as yet unpublished paper, has pointed out that Eph. 5.21f is concerned with a wife's submission to her husband in gratitude and love, as he is her 'head' or source of life (a contentious assumption for present day feminists, needless to say). The husband has no authority to command her, only to love her, nourish and cherish her. Dr McHugh has also looked carefully at the *Missale Romanum* of 1570, and the words *sit amabilis viro suo, ut Rachel: sapiens, ut Rebecca: longaeva et fidelis, ut Sarah* — loving and amiable to her husband as Rachel; wise, as Rebecca; and longlived and faithful, as Sarah. It was in the 1549 Prayer Book that 'longlived' was replaced by 'obedient', thus altering the whole sense of the climax of the blessing. See also Jean Laporte, *The Role of Women in Early Christianity* (New York, Edwin Mellen, 1982), pp. 46–51, Chrysostom's Homily 20 on Ephesians 5.22–4.

17   Taylor, *New Jerusalem*, p. 97.

18   Susan Brooks Thistlethwaite, 'Every Two Minutes: Battered Women and Feminist Interpretation', in Russell, op. cit., pp. 96–110.

19   George Egerton, *Keynotes and Discords* (Virago 1983); and see also Patricia Stubbs, *Women and Fiction: Feminism and the Novel, 1880–1920* (Methuen 1979).

20   Egerton, 'Virgin Soil', p. 157.

21   ibid. p. 155.

22   Taylor, *New Jerusalem*, p. 146.

23   ibid. p. 153.

24   Forster, *Significant Sisters*, p. 147.

25   Olive Schreiner, *The Story of an African Farm* (Penguin 1982).

26   ibid., p. 189.

27   Mary Daly, Gyn/Ecology (Women's Press 1984).

28   See Ruth First and Ann Scott, *Olive Schreiner* (Deutsch 1980); Liz Stanley, 'Olive Schreiner: New Women, Free Women, All Women (1855–1920)', in Dale Spender, *Feminist Theories* (Women's Press 1983), pp. 229–43.

29   Uys Krige, *Olive Schreiner: A Selection* (Oxford University Press 1986), p. 19.

30   ibid. p. 75.

31   First and Scott, *Olive Schreiner*, p. 263.

32 Schreiner, *African Farm*, p. 190.

33 ibid., p. 192.

34 ibid., p. 195-6.

35 ibid., p. 242.

36 See the chapter on her in Forster, *Significant Sisters*; Nancy Boyd, *Josephine Butler, Octavia Hill, Florence Nightingale: Three Victorian Women who Changed their World* (Macmillan 1982); and Alison Milbank, 'Josephine Butler: Christianity, Feminism and Social Action', in Jim Obelkevich, Lyndal Roper, Raphael Samuel (eds.), *Disciplines of Faith: Studies in Religion, Politics and Patriarchy* (Routledge & Kegan Paul 1987), pp. 154-64.

37 William Leach, *True Love and Perfect Union: The Feminist Reform of Sex and Society* (Routledge & Kegan Paul 1981), p. 40.

38 Henry Scott Holland, *A Bundle of Memories* (Wells, Gardner, Darton & Co. 1915), pp. 288-90.

39 Elizabeth Cady Stanton, *The Woman's Bible* (Polygon 1985), p. 119. See also Leach, *True Love and Perfect Union*, pp. 143-52; and Elisabeth Griffin, *In Her Own Right: The Life of Elizabeth Cady Stanton* (Oxford University Press 1984).

41 Cady Stanton, *The Woman's Bible*, p. 110.

42 ibid., 2, 19-20.

43 Erlene Stetson, 'Silence: Access and Aspirations' in Carole Ascher, Louise DeSalvo, Sara Ruddick (eds.), *Between Women* (Boston, Beacon Press, 1984), pp. 237-51, esp. p. 248.

44 Dorothy C. Bass, 'Women's Studies and Biblical Studies: An Historical Perspective' in *Journal for the Study of the Old Testament* 22 (1982), pp. 6-12.

45 Phyllis Trible, 'Biblical Theology as Women's Work' in *Religion in Life* 44 (1975), pp. 7-13.

46 Donald G. Mathews, 'Women's History/Everyone's History' in *Quarterly Review*, 1:5 (1981), pp. 41-60, esp. no. 18, p. 60.

47 E. M. Forster, *A Room with a View* (Penguin 1986), pp. 60-1.

2

THE LEAVEN OF MEMORY

Rediscovering the feminine in Christian tradition

The transforming action of a woman leavening bread dough is one of the many New Testament parables for the transforming presence of the divine reign within the constraints of domestic life. We might even think that the parable could refer to women's leavening the dough of the Church. I use the parable at this point to signal women's interest in the non-biblical resources of experience within Christian history, to see what they may have to offer women, both positively, by enabling the transformation which needs to take place, and negatively, by helping to identify what has to be repudiated. To engage in this kind of critical exercise is to try to pick out some features of women's experience within the Christian Church, and in comment on the phrase 'women's experience', I draw on some remarks by Nicola Slee:

> In practice, of course, women's experience is always specific to a particular social, cultural and historical situation: gender interacts with race, class, education and other social factors to shape the particular experience of being female, whether it is that of an educated middleclass European professional woman, for example, or the experience of an illiterate, third world, agricultural-working peasant woman. Given such radically differing particularisations of women's experience, and the unlikelihood of being able to generalise about all of them in terms appropriate to any, it may seem highly misleading to use the term at all. Nevertheless, feminist analysis argues that, without denying or ignoring the complex factors which interact to produce such differing expressions of women's lives, there remains an underlying unity of experience forged by women's common physiological nature and by a shared history and present experience of oppression and powerlessness. Within the terms of such analysis, to speak of 'women's experience' serves the dual function of both affirming that common reality of experience and attempting to redress the imbalance perpetuated by a system in which the dominant forms of thought and expression are determined by and reflect the needs of the socially powerful gender group and where, consequently, the needs and experiences of women are often forgotten, ignored, or, at best, subsumed under categories created by and appropriate to men.[1]

My starting point and conclusion is going to be with Dorothy

18

Sayers, as theologian, dramatist, translator of Dante amongst others, as well as creator of Lord Peter Wimsey and his Harriet. Christ, Dante and Lord Peter Wimsey are a formidable collection of heroes, and I draw in this chapter only on her work in respect of the first two. In 1946 she put together and published a collection of essays[2] that she had written and delivered in the previous ten years, and in this collection she begins to capture for us the problem of using non-biblical tradition as a resource. First of all, she had her own clear understanding of the Gospels and of their central character, totally without benefit of the insights of feminist theology of the kind with which we are beginning to become familiar, for the simple reason that in her day it did not exist, except in so far as women like her were talented enough to engage in it in their own way. Her view of Jesus and his relationships with women seems to survive scrutiny, even in comparison with the exegesis of Ben Witherington's *Women in the Ministry of Jesus*,[3] for example, though she does not employ his exegetical techniques, and might not have wished to do so, even had they been available to her. She had something else to offer, which was her talent as a dramatist.

She had in 1941 written a series of radio plays, which seem to have caused as much controversy in their own day as the television series 'Jesus, the evidence' did in the 1980s, called *The Man Born to be King*.[4] In these she had come to grips with the texts of the Gospels as they now stand, and with what she understood to be their realism, a realism which would survive vigorous translation into modern speech and into a new dramatic form. Amongst other things, she was doing what everyone has to do, which is to infer Jesus' attitudes towards women from the narratives in the Gospels of his encounters with them. Much too can be inferred about their role and status within early Christian communities from the way in which the writers of the Gospels deliver these narratives to their readers. Some of Dorothy Sayers' essays in her 1946 collection make the points that she conveyed in her dramatization, and it is not without significance that the first essay is on 'Christian morality'. In this essay, her opening remarks were as follows:

> Setting aside the scandal caused by His Messianic claims and His reputation as a political firebrand, only two accusations of personal depravity seem to have been brought against Jesus of Nazareth. First,

that He was a Sabbath-breaker. Secondly, that He was 'a gluttonous man and a winebibber, a friend of publicans and sinners' or ... that He ate too heartily, drank too freely, and kept very disreputable company, including grafters of the lowest type and ladies who were no better than they should be.[5]

Then she added: 'For nineteen and a half centuries, the Christian Churches have laboured, not with success, to remove this unfortunate impression made by their Lord and Master.' What was all too often left was unreality, in many expositions of the New Testament, dramatic or otherwise, where what one found was that, as she put it in her essay on 'Divine Comedy', 'The Humanity is never really there—it is always just coming on, or just going off, or being a light or a shadow or a voice in the wings.'[6] For her, Jesus was never a bore,[7] and she claimed that 'He was emphatically not a dull man in His human lifetime, and if He was God, there can be nothing dull about God either.'[8]

This daughter of a clerical family and of Anglo-Catholic persuasion had been nourished on the tough intellectual diet of 1662 Anglican Matins and Evensong and had learned her Christology accordingly. Defective Christology had at least two disastrous consequences. One was an insipid understanding of the Christian life. Question: 'What are the seven Christian virtues?' Answer: 'Respectability; childishness; mental timidity; dullness; sentimentality; censoriousness; and depression of spirits.'[9] The second was an uneasy understanding of women, which she tackled in her essay 'The human-not-quite-human', where she began:

> The first thing that strikes the careless observer is that women are unlike men. They are 'the opposite sex'—(though why 'opposite' I do not know; what is the 'neighbouring sex'?) But the fundamental thing is that women are more like men than anything else in the world. They are human beings. *Vir* is male and *Femina* is female: but *Homo* is male and female.
> This is the equality claimed and the fact that is persistently evaded and denied. No matter what arguments are used, the discussion is vitiated from the start, because Man is always dealt with as both *Homo* and *Vir*, but woman only as *Femina*.[10]

In Jesus of Nazareth Dorothy Sayers found no defective understanding of women.

> A prophet and teacher who never nagged at them, never flattered or

coaxed or patronised; who never made arch jokes about them, never treated them either as 'The women, God help us!' or 'The ladies, God bless them'; who rebuked without querulousness and praised without condescension; who took their questions and arguments seriously; who never mapped out their sphere for them, never urged them to be feminine or jeered at them for being female; who had no axe to grind and no uneasy male dignity to defend; who took them as he found them and was completely unselfconscious.[11]

In her opinion there was no act, no sermon, no parable in the whole Gospel that borrowed its pungency from female perversity, so that no one could possibly guess from Jesus' words and deeds that there was anything 'funny' about woman's nature. She thought, however, that it might be deduced from his contemporaries, and from his Church to this day. So she concluded: 'Women are not human; nobody shall persuade that they are human; let them say what they like, we will not believe it, though one rose from the dead.' She wanted recognition and appreciation of a shared human nature, *Homo*, on the part of both *Vir* and *Femina*.

What sort of tradition is it to which she is referring? Both the biblical texts and the texts which are more or less contemporary with those now to be found in the New Testament,[12] tell us a great deal about the uneasy and problematic transition of the original Christian communities with their revolutionary message of reconciliation and freedom into clear definition as organizations with institutional expression in the Graeco-Roman world. It seems clear enough that there was no final compromise on the value of women in the sense of appreciating their spiritual achievements, or with respect to their presumed destiny. Above all, some of the earliest documents exhibit the courage of women as martyrs, and Perpetua, martyred in AD 203 with her slave Felicitas, left her own account of her ordeal of imprisonment and of her visions, probably one of the earliest pieces of Christian literature from a woman of which we can be reasonably sure.[13] She left behind her a small son, not yet weaned when she was first imprisoned, and Felicitas walked into the arena only days after giving birth to her daughter after eight months of pregnancy. 'The mob was horrified, seeing that one was a charming girl, the other a woman lately risen from childbirth, with dripping breasts. So they were called back and clad in loose garments.'[14] Women also appear in the earliest traditions as

21

contemplatives, as prophets, as members of the order of widows (though quite what that amounted to is never likely to be very clear), as deacons and deaconnesses[15] and, importantly, as virgins.

For early Christianity offered women who did not or could not fulfil certain socio-sexual roles, a new kind of aspiration. Women who found the roles of wife and mother inadequate measures of their worth, or who could not participate in the undoubted rewards to be found in those roles, found the claims of discipleship which went back to Jesus of Nazareth taking overriding priority in their lives.[16] To be single and sexually virginal was to be freed from a measure of male domination and from the perils of childbearing. It is simply a mistake to think of sexual asceticism as necessarily imposed on them as a kind of constraint. Well into the medieval period and beyond there were worse fates than the retreat to a book-lined cell.[17] There is one very interesting story available to us from the seventeenth century, about Elena Lucrezia Cornaro Piscopia, a Venetian— admittedly she was probably exceptional in the support she was given by her patrician family—who had refused everything except the life of a Benedictine oblate in her parental home, and who at the age of thirty-one qualified to receive her doctorate in theology. The bishop of Padua intervened, since the degree would have given her the right to teach theology, and as the writer of 1 Timothy 2.11–12 says, 'Let a woman learn in silence with all submissiveness. I permit no woman to teach or to have authority over men; she is to keep silent.' Elena's father negotiated a compromise and the degree was awarded in philosophy. After her *viva voce* examination, she seems to have retreated into privacy, but we could say that she and her family had made their point.[18]

Virginity, with or without the book-lined cell, did not and does not necessarily connect with what has been called a 'stony asexuality',[19] or with bizarre or self-destructive behaviour, though sometimes it may do, as we can see in the next chapter. Dorothy Sayers produced for *Punch* in 1954 a good example of a 'spoof saint' of this kind, St Supercilia, patron saint of pedants, born in Paris about 1400. She was

> a maiden of remarkable erudition, who steadfastly refused to marry anyone who could not defeat her in open disputation. When all the best scholars of all the universities in Europe had tried and failed, her

unworthy father brutally commanded her to accept the hand of a man who, though virtuous, sensible, and of a good estate, knew only six languages and was weak in mathematics. At this, the outraged saint raised her eyebrows so high that they lifted her right off her feet and out through a top-storey window, where she was last seen floating away in a northerly direction.[20]

However, Margaret Brennan, an Immaculate Heart of Mary Sister, has also been led to wonder whether the exaltation that was accorded to the life of perpetual virginity in women 'did not come in part from the fact that consecrated virginity also removed women from their proximity to men. It diminished their power as temptress or at least as sources of distraction in the pursuance of a disembodied spirituality.'[21] Thus the appeal and power of Christian sexual asceticism came to influence injunctions to widows and even to women still actually married. We know how Jerome, for instance, made up his sexual score-card in relation to the one-hundred-fold harvest in the parable of the sower—the hundred-fold harvest indicated virginity, sixty-fold indicates widowhood, and the thirty-fold marriage.[22] So he wrote to one widow, whom he was encouraging to remain *un*married:

> Have about you troops of virgins whom you may lead into the King's chamber. Support widows that you may mingle them as a kind of violet with the virgin's lilies and the martyr's roses. Such are the garlands you must weave for Christ in place of that cross of thorns in which he bore the sins of the world.[23]

The flower imagery turns up again in a ninth-century lament for a young abbess, another Heloise, as Helen Waddell said. (Helen Waddell was the daughter of an Irish Presbyterian missionary family, whose spiritual nourishment as writer and translator was found in the Latin western tradition. Herself a life-long, though somewhat unwilling, celibate, she was greatly beloved and a great lover of others, and not only wrote *Peter Abelard* but translated *Manon Lescaut* too.) The lament for a young abbess she translated during the bombing raids of September 1941, which makes it all the more poignant:

> Thou has come safe to port,
> I still at sea,
> The light is on thy head,
> Darkness in me.

23

Pluck thou in heaven's field
Violet and rose,
While I strew flowers that will thy vigil keep,
Where thou dost sleep,
Love, in thy last repose.[24]

We can add to that her translation of an eleventh-century verse about the virgins in the fields of the Blessed, like the girls illustrated in Fra Angelico's picture of St Thomas Aquinas and St Bonaventura talking together in Paradise:

Gertrude, Agnes, Prisca, Cecily,
Lucia, Thekla, Petronel,
Agatha, Barbara, Juliana,
Wandering there in the fresh spring meadows,
Looking for flowers to make them a garland,
Roses red of the Passion,
Lilies and violets for love.[25]

This material helps to make intelligible why the habit grew up of defining women in terms of their sexuality, a habit which as Janet Morley has so wittily pointed out can seem so exasperating, and is still exhibited, for instance, in the list of lesser saints in the Church of England's new Alternative Services Book. Clare of Assisi is designated as a virgin, Josephine Butler as a social reformer, wife and mother; this is exasperating when no comparable sexual distinctions are accorded to the men, even when we know that they were husbands and fathers.[26]

But we still have not accounted for Dorothy Sayers' problem with the tradition, which has to do with practical misogyny, as well as with the disparagement of those women who were not virgins. It is difficult, to put it mildly, to assess the rhetoric of misogyny, not least in the Christian context. One point of which we might take notice is made by Dom Jean Leclercq in his book *The Love of Learning and the Desire for God*, where he refers to what might be called 'literary exaggeration'. On this he comments:

It accounts for much in the ancients' works and is quite in keeping since these men are, so to speak, 'learned primitives'. As primitives— and the word in this context has no pejorative connotation—they think one thing at a time, experience one feeling at a time, but they think and feel intensely. They have little in common with those complex individuals whose every psychological reaction interferes immediately with another which tempers and modifies it.[27]

24

Misogyny can be a defensive strategy in response to real or supposed power, including the power to deceive and to humiliate, but Helen Waddell is surely right to have spotted that 'It is not the man whose senses are blunt who makes the sternest ascetic.'[28]

> Who is this
> That knockest at the gate,
> Breaking the sleep of the night?
> That crieth
> O of all virgins fairest,
> Sister, bride,
> Gem that is rarest.
> Rise, O rise,
> Open sweetest.[29]

That is her translation of a hymn to the Blessed Virgin Mary by Peter Damian, ferocious in his austerity. Another example comes from the dramas of Hrotsvit a tenth-century canoness of the Saxon Imperial Abbey of Gandersheim, who sought, as Dr Katharina Wilson has said in her introduction to her translation of Hrotsvit's dramas, 'to gain both intellectual and emotional assent to the monastic ideal'.[30] And further, 'Her courageous undertaking is the fruit not only of her natural genius, her education, environment and profession, but also of her intellectual, emotional and religious adherence to the moral responsibility and exalted role of the Christian preacher.' This first poet of Saxony, first female German poet, the first dramatist of Germany, wrote for performance, probably in the form of dramatic recitation, and this particular example comes from 'The Conversion of General Gallicanus'. Promised the hand of a daughter of Constantine, he finds that she cannot marry him because she has taken a vow of chastity. He too becomes a Christian and renounces marriage:

Gallicanus: Had I not been changed for the better,
I would not have given my consent to your vow, no, never.

Constancia: May the Friend of virginal modesty, Patron of all good will, He who held you back from your unlawful intention and claimed my virginity for Himself, reward our separation here on earth with uniting us above in everlasting mirth.

Gallicanus:	May that come to be!
Constantinus:	Since the tie of Christ's love unites us in the fellowship of one religion, it is proper that you, the Emperor's son-in-law, live honourably in the palace with me.
Gallicanus:	No temptation is to be shunned more, Sire, than the eyes' wanton desire.
Constantinus:	I cannot contradict that.
Gallicanus:	Therefore I am afraid to behold frequently the very maid whom, as you know I love above my parents, my life, my very soul and ease.[31]

Helen Waddell's comment was, 'It is not the speech of the plaster saint'.[32] Elsewhere, she put her finger on another problem arising from monastic asceticism, admirable though it could and can be. In her book *The Desert Fathers* (1936), she sums up one of the points of asceticism by saying, 'Human passion, the passion of anger as well as of lust, entangled the life of the spirit: therefore passion must be dug out by the roots'.[33] Ascetics were admired not so much for their discipline as for much harder virtues, such as magnanimity, humility, gentleness, 'heartbreaking courtesy',[34] and the tenderness expressed in the story of St Macarius who gave sight to the blind whelp of a hyaena who brought it to him in her mouth.[35] Helen Waddell quoted George Meredith, no Puritan, as saying, 'Spirit must brand the flesh that it may live', and quotes it again in her introduction to the lives of the harlots converted to Christianity and therefore in their case to sexual asceticism (Thaïs, Pelagia, Mary of Egypt), and this time to Meredith's saying, she adds the question, 'but what if the branding become a cancer?'[36]

The cancerous element in asceticism so far as women were concerned is displayed above all in the story of Thaïs, courtesan of Alexandria converted by Paphnutius, who shut her up in a one-room cell. In Hrotsvit's version:

Thaïs:	What could be more unsuitable what could be more uncomfortable, than that I would have to perform all necessary functions of the body in the very same room? I am sure that it will soon be uninhabitable because of the stench.

Pafnutius: Fear rather the eternal tortures of Hell,
              and not the transitory inconveniences of your cell.

Thaïs: My frailty makes me afraid.

Pafnutius: It is only right
              that you expatiate the evil sweetness of alluring delight
              by enduring this terrible smell.

Thaïs: And so I shall.
              I, filthy myself, do not refuse to dwell
              in a filthy befouled cell
              —that is my just due.
              But it pains me deeply that there is no spot left dignified
              and pure,
              where I could invoke the name of God's majesty.

Pafnutius: And how can you have such great confidence that you
              would presume to utter the name of the unpolluted
              Divinity with your polluted lips?

Thaïs: But how can I hope for grace, how can I be saved by His
              mercy if I am not allowed to invoke Him, against Whom
              alone I sinned, and to Whom alone I should offer my
              devotion and prayer?

Pafnutius: Clearly you should pray not with words but with tears;
              not with your tinkling voice's melodious art
              but with the bursting of your penitent heart.

Paphnutius' parting shot to Thaïs' abbess is
'I commit my charge to your care and kindness
so that you may nourish her delicate body with a few necessities
occasionally
and nourish her soul with profitable admonitions frequently.' No
Josephine Butler, one feels, the Abbess promises to look after
her, 'and my maternal affections will never cease.'[37] Paphnutius
left her in her cell for three years and extracted her from it,
although she had all too hideously become accustomed to it, only
in time to die. Helen Waddell commented that in this story
Paphnutius is a figure for the vengeance of God and man, and
refers us to Anatole France's version of it, since she rightly says
that it is a credit to France that his gorge rose at it, and that he
understood the Nemesis that waits upon the absolute denial of
the body. In France's version he makes Paphnutius *himself* the
target of the demons of pride, lust and doubt, and his final words

27

are, 'He had become so repulsive, that passing his hand over his face, he felt his own hideousness.'[38]

There are, fortunately, also a few stories from the Desert Fathers which make it clear that both monastic and non-monastic women were not always perceived in misogynistic ways, and that they could be seen to embody admirable qualities, not the least the ability to encourage monks to maintain their commitment to celibacy. Dom Columba Stewart has recently made these available in translation[39]—and there were some 'Desert Mothers', of whom we have a few accounts. But the legacy was a long one: 'A certain nun, fair after the putridity of the flesh', love too near 'the sweetest sin of the seven' to be much countenanced, and marriage as 'the last shift'.[40] Rare indeed, as Marina Warner has pointed out, was the defence of women in terms of their *resemblance* to the Virgin Mary, of which an example is found in the reply of a nightingale to a misogynist thrush in a thirteenth-century English discussion:

> Man's highest bliss in earthly state
> Is when a woman takes her mate
> And twines him in her arms,
> To slander ladies is a shame![41]

Almost effaced from memory was the *authority* of Mary of Magdala as witness of the resurrection and therefore 'apostle to the apostles' by the Western Church's habit of identifying her with other 'Mary's' in the Gospel, and above all with the woman who was a 'great sinner'. Take one example of the confusion:

> Mary was mother of the Lord,
> And Lazarus' sister was a Mary too,
> Both bright heavens to befriend men's souls.
> The handmaid no way equal to her lady
> But shares her radiant name.
>
> The one is the very symbol of repentance,
> The other the mother of all pardon.
> The one was the virgin of virgins, saint of all saints,
> The other had known all sin and company kept with sinners.
> One Mary bore the feet that the other held, weeping,
> And because she greatly loved she was purified of her stain....

To her the risen Lord had first shown himself
And made his first apostle.
A woman of ill fame.[42]

It is one of the curiosities of Christian history that a woman who had been mentally ill and was one of those with whom Jesus seems to have had a specially loving relationship, was robbed of her apostolic authority not least by her association with the 'penitent whores' of the tradition, as well as simply by the fact that she was merely a woman. In one Latin interpretation of the encounter of Mary with the risen Christ, the writer argued that she was forbidden to touch him because her faith in the resurrection had wavered. Peter and John go in to the tomb, and far from weeping, run away rejoicing. 'Only she who did not enter wept, and in her disbelief she thought the body had been carried off deceitfully.' It is a woman who did not believe, 'for the one who believes, rises to *perfect manhood, to the measure of the stature of the fulness of Christ'*. Her lack of faith is contrasted with that of the faith of the Virgin Mary who had already believed. 'When she does not believe, she is "woman"; when she begins to be converted, she is called "Mary", that is, she receives the name of her who bore Christ. For a holy soul can be said to bear Christ spiritually.' She is instructed to go to ask 'more perfect men' to explain to her the distinction between 'my Father and your Father'.[43] If we recover Mary of Magdala as an apostle and preacher, we need not lose sight of her as a lover, disentangled from the idea of her as 'a sensuously erotic makeweight' as Elisabeth Moltmann-Wendel puts it.[44] Dorothy Day was a social radical and convert to Roman Catholicism, not infrequently in prison with prostitutes, drug addicts, forgers and thieves, who showed to her and her co-workers more loving-kindness than did their jailers. Yet she once failed to 'see Christ' in a disturbed girl who tried to make a sexual attack on Judith, a co-worker imprisoned with Dorothy Day. It was for the girl that she could, as it were, pray on the feast of St Mary Magdalene using the language from the Song of Songs in the 1570 Roman Missal:

On my bed at night I sought Him
Whom my heart loves—
I sought Him but I did not find Him.

29

I will rise then and go about the city;
   in the streets and crossings I will seek
Him whom my heart loves.
I sought Him but I did not find Him...

Oh, that You were my brother,
   nursed at my mother's breasts!
If I met You out of doors, I would kiss You
   and none would taunt me.
I would lead You, bring You in
   to the home of my mother...

Rejoice with me, all you who love the Lord, for
I sought Him and He appeared to me. And while I
   was weeping at the tomb, I saw my Lord,
   Alleluia.[45]

Misogyny could be born of hostility, possibly unconscious, to women who are, or who have been, sexually active, and it could ally itself intellectually with erroneous biology (maybe the best available, but erroneous nonetheless). A dominant tradition in biology regarded the male as the normative and representative expression of the human species, with the female as deformed or imperfect human being. In some cases, women were thought to be useful only for procreation; otherwise men were thought to be more generally useful and better company, so if procreation were not in view, women were likely to be defined as nuisances.[46] It is no longer possible to ignore the arguments about the sense in which women could or could not be regarded as being *in themselves* bearers of the divine 'image' in humanity, as *Homo* rather than as *Vir*, so 'godlike' as men were deemed to be.[47] The significance is more in the fact that there should have been such arguments at all, rather than in the particular conclusions to which theologians came, unless these are nowadays to be regarded as normative. The concept of 'paternity' is a crucial element in the discussion too, to which I shall return in my last chapter.

For the moment we can notice the sexual virginity in women was at least one sign of defiance of what seemed to be the 'natural' order of things; that spirituality and the practice of the virtues were associated primarily with males, except in so far as women could approximate to masculinity; that discomfort with bodiliness could express itself in anger at women who accidently and yet insistently reminded men of their embodiment; so the stage is as it were set for the Tertullians of this world. Yet why is his much-quoted remark that woman is the 'devil's gateway' to be found in his treatise on the dress of women which dates from the early years of the third century?[48] Women in his view were to wear the dress of penitence for being the first forsakers of the divine law, and he argues that 'because of *your* punishment, that is death, even the Son of God had to die'. Rosemary Radford Ruether is on target when she says that since woman is associated with all the sensual and depraved characteristics of mind through her bodiliness as seen from the male visual perspective, 'her salvation must be seen not as an affirmation of her nature but as a negation of her nature, both physically and mentally, and a transformation into a possibility beyond her natural capacities'.[49] Thus Ambrose of Milan:

> Speak to Christ, alone, converse with Christ alone. For if *women should keep silence in church*, how much more unfitting it is for a virgin to open her door, for a widow to open her courtyard. How quickly the waylayer of modesty creeps up, how quickly he elicits the word you would have wanted to recall.

> If Eve's door had been closed, Adam would not have been deceived and she, under question, would not have responded to the serpent. Death entered through the window, i.e. through the door of Eve. And death will come in through your door if you speak falsely, lasciviously, or impudently especially when there is no call upon you to speak. Therefore, let the gates of your lips be closed and the vestibule of your voice remain bolted; then, perhaps they will be unbolted when you hear the voice of God, when you hear the Word of God.

Not surprisingly then,

> she who seeks Christ ought not to be well known; she should not be in the square or in the streets with tremulous voice, an easy stride, a ready ear, and a vulgar appearance. The Apostle denies earthly society to you, instructing you to fly to heaven on spiritual wings, almost beyond the limits of nature.[50]

Rosemary Radford Ruether comments that the redeemed woman has not only to subject her body and personality but also abase her 'visual image', so that she will in no way appear in the body as a woman before the eyes of the male. Hence the interest in the Fathers with matters of physical appearance, and the response of some women by retreat into seclusion and sometimes male attire. Jill Raitt has recently published a very perceptive article in the *Journal of the American Academy of Religion*[51] more precisely on the phrase 'the devil's gateway', by associating it with some of the myths to be found in folk literature of the *vagina dentata*—the vagina with teeth—the terror of castration or sexual humiliation in face of the supposed sexual insatiability of women (one of the oldest jokes in the world). It was no joke, however, when women as the devil's gateway turned up hideously in later centuries in the context of the witchhunts. In the *Malleus Maleficarum*, which has to do with *female* evil-doers, we can find this assertion:

> All witchcraft comes from carnal lust, which is in women insatiable. See Proverbs xxx: there are three things that are never satisfied, yea a fourth thing which says not, 'It is enough: that is, the *mouth* of the womb. Wherefore for the sake of fulfilling their lusts they consort even with devils'.

To that we could add Jean-Paul Sartre's observations on the female sex, his symbol of the material world, which for him was as alien to intellect and will as for some of the Fathers.

> I want to let go of the slimy and it sticks to me, it draws me, it sucks at me ... It is a soft, yielding action, a moist and feminine sucking ... it draws me to it as the bottom of a precipice might draw me ... A sickly-sweet, feminine revenge ... The obscenity of the feminine sex is that of everything which 'gapes open'. It is *an appeal to being*, as all holes are .... Beyond any doubt her sex is a mouth and a voracious mouth which devours the penis.[52]

As we take stock of these habits of thought, we need both to approve and develop the sense of transcendence and personality some women found in Christianity, and discard and condemn any association of those values with inhuman denigration not only of the humanity of women, but of the affections of both sexes for one another. So far, however, I hope that I have said enough to indicate how, in alliance with the development of feminine symbolism for the Church as bride and mother[53] (which I shall not discuss), church structures would inevitably exclude women. If women were not regarded as fully human except insofar as they could approximate to men, and they could not actually become men, they could be fairly represented by men, and to so change one's evaluation of women should imply some change in church structures. There would have to be clearly defensible reasons for not doing so at certain points if structures are to remain much as they are, and it is no good appealing to such an ambivalent tradition for the legitimation of the *status quo*: women are God's creation and yet the curse of the world; weak and intellectually defective, yet they could display great courage, and some of them became great scholars—and so on.

Before moving on to some other points that I want to make about the tradition, I should like to quote one unconsciously comic passage on one of those scholars, from Jerome's praise of the learning of Marcella, a Roman widow profoundly influenced by the traditions of the Egyptian Desert Fathers. I am quoting it as an example of how even learned and ascetic women could find it almost impossible to claim who and what they were for themselves. Jerome wrote:

> Thus after my departure, if an argument arose about some evidence from Scripture, the question was pursued with her as the judge. And because she was so discreet and knew about... 'how to behave appropriately', when she was thus questioned, she used to reply as if what was said was not her own, but came either from me or from another man, in order to confess that about the matters she was teaching, she herself had been a pupil. For she knew the saying of the Apostle, 'I do not, however, permit a woman to teach' (1 Tim. 2.12), lest she seem to inflict an injury on the male sex and on those priests who were enquiring about obscure and difficult points.[54]

What Marcella needed to be in a position to do was to go on claiming scholarship as a form of intellectual asceticism, as in some forms of the monastic tradition, but to be able to claim her results for herself. In one sense one might say that her successors in pure scholarship are women like the two Smith sisters, Agnes and Maggie, a pair of identical twins of Scots Presbyterian stock.[55] They made their first trip back to the world closest to that of Jerome, one might say, in 1868, and there found their reason for existence in scholarship as a kind of religious exercise rather by chance. They had become the sort of women of whom even Jerome might have approved, with Hebrew, Arabic and Syriac between them, and as widows went on expeditions to the library in the Monastery of St Catherine in the mountains of the Sinai peninsula. When they visited the library in 1892 to pursue their researches, they happened one day to look rather carefully at the vellum used for serving butter on at their meals. Finding the text from which it was a portion, they discovered the top layer of writing to be what Agnes published as 'Select Narratives of Holy Women'—a strange link as it were between women from such very different cultures. (Some of these narratives are now being republished in a new Canadian journal called *Vox Benedictina* and the same publishers are responsible for a series of translations called *Matrologia Latina*, all of which will familiarize us with this and other forgotten material about women.) The underneath layer of writing happened to be a copy of gospel material in Syriac—now known as the Lewis Syriac Gospels—and the text may go back to the second century. Their situation was unlike that of Marcella; even the learned world could by this time acknowledge their scholarship. In 1899 Agnes received the degrees of Doctor of Philosophy and Master of Liberal Arts from Halle as the discoverer of the Codex. Both sisters received degrees of Doctor of Law from St Andrews in 1904 and degrees of Doctor of Divinity from Heidelberg. These were the first theological doctorates to be conferred upon women by any university in the world, with Litt.Ds to follow from Trinity College, Dublin in 1911. Here at long last was scholarship in women properly honoured, though still extraordinary in the United Kingdom. The University of Cambridge, situated in the town where they had chosen to live, and with essential academic friends there, could not give them so much as an honorary MA. Durham, in its University Act of 1908, was prepared to admit women to degrees in any faculty save theology. When Dorothy Sayers took her Oxford BA and MA together in 1920 (not of course as a theologian), in the first batch of women to be permitted to do so, it was the first time the Latin *domina* had been addressed to graduates in that University.

Since I began with her in this chapter, I should like to go back to her, as an example of someone trying to live out the implications of a full-blooded Christology,[56] but bearing in mind a remark of Dom Louis Leloir's. Writing of 'Women and the Desert Fathers' he draws attention to the reality that there exists both the danger of loving too much and of loving too little, and that the Fathers were especially afraid of the former, whereas we on the other hand fear the latter, despite our knowledge of human weakness.[57] Dorothy Sayers knew all about what she called the 'passionate intellect', the only point for her at which she said ecstasy could enter. 'I do not know whether we can be saved through the intellect, but I do know that I can be saved by nothing else.' She added:

> I know that, if there is judgement, I shall have to be able to say: 'This alone, Lord, in Thee and in me, have I never betrayed, and may it suffice to know and love and choose Thee after this manner, for I have no other love, or knowledge, or choice in me'.[58]

To say, however, that Dorothy Sayers lived a purely intellectual life so far as she could would be a distortion of the facts. She refused a Lambeth DD partly because she did not want too close an association of her work with apologetic theology and partly because she did not want to cause scandal to her church, since on the one hand, on the rebound from one love affair she had conceived and given birth to a son outside marriage, and on the other, she had married a divorced man in a registry office.

When she began to translate and to write essays on Dante's *Divine Comedy* in 1944 onwards, it was perhaps inevitable that she would be captivated by Dante's love for Beatrice and see its theological significance in its satisfaction both of emotion and intellect. She saw in this love something of what Helen Waddell had noticed first in the reaction to Pelagia's beauty by Bishop Nonnus, who converted her. Nonnus himself was one of those known as *Amantissimus Dei*—a great lover of God, *nimirum* beyond question—and he alone saw in Pelagia the beauty which should judge him and his episcopate.[59] Dante recognized that

> Yet, as a wheel turns equal, free from jars,
> Already my will and desire were wheeled by love,
> The Love that moves the sun and the other stars,[60]

and it was this love which consumed him when he received Beatrice's greeting. He could then forgive all who had ever injured him, and 'if at that moment I had been questioned of anything whatsoever, I should have answered simply *Love*, with a countenance clothed in humility'.[61] In the *Divine Comedy* negation gives way to affirmation, and when Dante sees Beatrice in the 'pageant of the sacrament'[62] in the company of the Christ-Gryphon (to signify the mystery of the divine and human) it is Beatrice who comes as Christ's bride-Church and it is to *her* that the sacramental greeting is given, 'Benedictus qui venis',[63] that is,

'Blessed (m.) art thou that comest'. So Dorothy Sayers concludes that 'Beatrice is the particular type and image of that whole sacramental principle of which the Host itself is the greater Image... she is Sacrament', which for Dorothy Sayers meant 'the manifestation of the Divine Glory in whatsoever beloved thing becomes to every man his own particular sacramental principle'.[64] So what is wanted at the very least is the recognition that 'we draw one another up by a continual exchange, passing one another, as it were, by turns upon the ladder of ascent, the higher always giving a hand to whoever is at the moment the lower'.[65]

Notes

1   Nicola Slee, 'Parables and Women's Experience' in *Modern Churchman*, 26:2 (1984), pp. 20–31, esp. pp. 21–2.

2   Dorothy L. Sayers, *Unpopular Opinions* (Gollancz 1946).

3   Ben Witherington III, *Women in the Ministry of Jesus: A Study of Jesus' Attitudes to Women and their Roles as Reflected in his Earthly Life* (Cambridge University Press 1984).

4   Dorothy L. Sayers, *The Man Born to be King* (Gollancz 1943).

5   Sayers, *Unpopular Opinions*, p. 9.

6   ibid., p. 21.

7   Dorothy L. Sayers, 'The Dogma is the Drama' in *Creed or Chaos and Other Essays in Popular Theology* (Methuen 1949), p. 24.

8   Quoted in James Brabazon, *Dorothy Sayers: The Life of a Courageous Woman* (Gollancz 1981), pp. 166–7, from the *Sunday Times* of April 1938, 'The greatest drama ever staged is the official creed of Christendom'.

9   'The Dogma is the Drama', p. 23.

10   Sayers, *Unpopular Opinions*, p. 116.

11   ibid., p. 122.

12   See particularly the passages from 'The Gospel of the Egyptians', 'The Gospel of Philip' and 'The Gospel of Thomas' cited in Rosemary Radford Ruether (ed.), *Womanguides: Readings towards a Feminist Theology* (Boston, Beacon Press, 1985) pp. 122–3; and Ron Cameron, *The Other Gospels: Non-Canonical Gospel Texts* (Philadelphia, Westminster Press, 1982). See also the bibliography in Ross S. Kraemer, 'Women in the Religions of the Greco-Roman World' in *Religious Studies Review*, 9:2 (April 1983), pp. 127–39.

13   Elizabeth A. Clark, *Women in the Early Church*, Message of the Fathers of the Church, 13 (Wilmington, Michael Glazier, 1983), pp. 97–106; Elizabeth Alvilda Petroff (ed.), *Medieval Women's Visionary Literature* (Oxford University Press 1985), pp. 70–7; and the discussion in Peter Dronke, *Women Writers of the Middle Ages* (Cambridge University Press 1984), pp. 1–16.

14   Clark, *Women in the Early Church*, p. 104.
15   Aimé Georges Martimort, *Deaconesses: An Historical Study* tr. K. D. Whitehead, (San Francisco, Ignatius Press, 1986).
16   Ross S. Kraemer, 'The conversion of Women to Ascetic Forms of Christianity' in *Signs*, 16:2 (1980), pp. 298–307.
17   Patricia H. Labalme (ed.), *Beyond Their Sex: Learned Women of the European Past* (New York University Press 1980), p. 4: 'An eloquent woman was reputedly unchaste; a learned lady threatened male pride. The book-lined cell... symbolized the retreat, at some cost, of many learned women from a hostile world.'
18   Labalme, 'Women's Roles in Early Modern Venice: An Exceptional Case' in Labalme, op. cit.
19   See Margaret L. King's essay, 'Book-lined Cells: Women and Humanism in the Early Italian Renaissance' in Labalme, op. cit., p. 78.
20   Brabazon, p. 258.
21   Margaret Brennan, 'Enclosure: Institutionalising the Invisibility of Women in Ecclesiastical Communities' in Elisabeth Schüssler Fiorenza and Mary Collins (eds.), *Women—Invisible in Theology and Church* (T. & T. Clark 1985), pp. 38–48, esp. p. 40.
22   Clark, *Women in the Early Church*, pp. 127f.
23   Jean Laporte, *The Role of Women in Early Christianity*, p. 69.
24   Dame Felicitas Corrigan, *Helen Waddell: A Biography* (Gollancz 1986), p. 317; and Dame Felicitas Corrigan (ed.), *More Latin Lyrics from Virgil to Milton*, tr. Helen Waddell (Gollancz 1976), pp. 224–5, esp. p. 225.
25   Helen Waddell, *The Wandering Scholars* (Penguin 1954), p. 123.
26   Janet Morley, '"The Faltering Words of Men": Exclusive Language in the Liturgy' in Monica Furlong (ed.), *Feminine in the Church* (SPCK 1984), pp. 56–70.
27   Jean Leclercq, *The Love of Learning and the Desire for God*, tr. Catharine Misrahi (New York, Fordham University Press, 1974), p. 166.
28   Waddell, *More Latin Lyrics*, p. 234.
29   ibid., pp. 236–7.
30   *The Dramas of Hrotsvit of Gandersheim*, tr. Katharina M. Wilson (Saskatoon, Matrologia Latina & Peregrina, 1985), p. 1.
31   ibid., p. 45.
32   Waddell, *The Wandering Scholars*, p. 101.
33   Helen Waddell, *The Desert Fathers* (Constable 1954), p. 14.
34   ibid., p. 17 and p. 29.
35   Helen Waddell, *Beasts and Saints* (Constable 1942), p. 13.
36   Waddell, *The Desert Fathers*, p. 261.
37   *Hrotsvit*, tr. Wilson, pp. 105–6.
38   Anatole France, *Thaïs*, tr. Robert B. Douglas (John Lane 1928), p. 249.
39   *The World of the Desert Fathers* tr. Columba Stewart (SLG Press 1986), pp. 13–18. See also his paper 'The Portrayal of Women in the Sayings and Stories of the Desert' in *Vox Benedictina*, 2:1, pp. 5–23.
40   Waddell, *The Wandering Scholars*, p. 229.
41   Marina Warner, *Alone of All her Sex* (Picador 1985) p. 153.

42   Waddell, *More Latin Lyrics*, pp. 244–5, by Marbod of Rennes.
43   Interpolations into *St Ambrose on Virginity*, tr. Daniel Callam (Saskatoon, Peregrina, 1980), from Paras. 15–23.
44   Elisabeth Moltmann-Wendel, *The Women around Jesus*, tr. John Bowden (SCM Press 1982), p. 88.
45   Robert Ellsberg (ed.), *By Little and by Little: The Selected Writings of Dorothy Day* (New York, Borzoi, 1983), pp. 292–3 (see Song of Sol. 3.1–2; 8.1–2); William D. Miller, *Dorothy Day: A Biography* (San Francisco, Harper & Row, 1982), pp. 438–40.
46   Ruether, *Womanguides*, sections 4–5.
47   Kari Elisabeth Børresen, *Subordination and Equivalence: The Nature and Role of Woman in Augustine and Thomas Aquinas*, tr. Charles H. Talbot (University Press of America 1981); 'Imago Dei, Privilège Masculin? Interprétation Augustinienne et pseudo-Augustinienne de Gen. 1.27 et 1 Cor. 11.7' *Augustinianum* 25 (1985), pp. 213–34; see also Henry Chadwick, *Augustine* (Oxford University Press 1986), pp. 89–90 for one brief summary.
48   Clark, *Women in the Early Church*, p. 39.
49   Rosemary Radford Ruether (ed.), *Religion and Sexism: Images of Woman in the Jewish and Christian Traditions* (New York, Simon and Schuster, 1974); her own essay 'Misogynism and Virginal Feminism in the Fathers of the Church', p. 161.
50   *On Virginity*, tr. Callam, from paras. 80–3.
51   Jill Raitt, 'The *Vagina Dentata* and the *Immaculatus Uterus Divini Fontis*' in *Journal of the American Academy of Religion*, 48 (September 1980), pp. 415–31. She comments that in the Hebrew context it is not 'carnal lust' which never says 'Enough!' but the desire of a barren woman to conceive.
52   Quoted in Midgley, 'Sex and Personal Identity', p. 54.
53   See for example Henri de Lubac, *The Motherhood of the Church*, tr. Sr Sergia Englund (San Francisco, Ignatius Press, 1982).
54   Clark, *Women in the Early Church*, p. 208.
55   A. Wigham-Price, *The Ladies of Castlebrae* (Sutton 1985).
56   See also Margaret P. Hannay, '"Through the World Like a Flame": Christology in the Dramas of Dorothy L. Sayers' in *Vox Benedictina*, 2:2 (1985), pp. 148–66.
57   Louis Leloir, 'Woman and the Desert Fathers' in *Vox Benedictina*, 3:3 (1986), pp. 207–27.
58   Brabazon, *Dorothy Sayers*, p. 263.
59   Waddell, *The Desert Fathers*, p. 263–4.
60   Dante, *Paradiso*, 33, pp. 143–5.
61   Dorothy L. Sayers, 'The Poetry of the Image in Dante and Charles Williams' in *Further Papers on Dante* (Methuen 1957), p. 189.
62   Dante, *Purgatorio* 29, pp. 106f.
63   ibid., 30, p. 19.
64   Sayers, 'The Poetry of the Image', p. 192.
65   ibid., p. 194.

3

CHRIST ALSO SUFFERED

Why certain forms of holiness are bad for you

Christianity has rarely taken on board Immanuel Kant's suspicion of examples in morality,[1] though the text Kant cited (Luke 18.19) is not the one (1 Pet. 2.21) used in my chapter title. Kant, like other major enlightenment philosophers, was rightly chary of doing more than indicating the meaning of Christ's death;[2] and Iris Murdoch more recently has shown us in the figure of the priest Cato in her novel *Henry and Cato*[3] just how easily the 'imitation of Christ' can be the expression of profound egotism, with disastrous consequences not only for the man involved but for those he tries to serve.

In my first chapter I cited Elisabeth Schüssler Fiorenza's warning label to be placed on all biblical texts: 'Caution! Could be dangerous to your health and survival!' and the text from 1 Peter is particularly interesting in this connection, assuming of course that women have an interest in health and survival for their own sakes as well as for the sake of living the 'resurrection' life of gospel promise. I also said that Elizabeth Cady Stanton takes us to the point of setting the present-day agenda of discovering new ways of interpreting some of the biblical texts which had been supposed to authorize women's subordination, and I referred to Phyllis Trible's argument for biblical theology as women's work, and for the movement in feminist theology, which argues—quite rightly, in my view—that centuries of certain habits of exegesis stand under judgement, and not just the traditions of exegesis, but the very texts themselves, without immunity. One group of examples I would like to mention at this point is particularly pertinent to my overall theme in this chapter. I refer to texts at which Elizabeth Cady Stanton jibbed. For example, she did not quite know what to do about interpreting the story of Tamar, except to omit it,[4] bearing in mind what she thought about the 'wholesale desecration of women and children' which was brought to light in Josephine Butler's campaigns. Elizabeth Cady Stanton did manage to express her anger at the story of 'Jephthah's daughter',[5] who, as she said, belonged to the 'no-name' series—and the victim was only a girl. 'So much glamour has been thrown by poetry and song, over the sacrifice of this Jewish maiden, that the popular mind has become too benumbed to perceive its great injustice.' She had rather 'this page of history were gilded with a dignified whole-souled rebellion', with the daughter rebuking the father:

> I will not consent to such a sacrifice. Your vow must be disallowed. You may sacrifice your own life as you please, but you have no right over mine. I am on the threshold of life, the joys of youth and of middle age are all before me. You are in the sunset; you have had your blessings and your triumphs; but mine are yet to come. Life to me is full of hope and of happiness. Better that you die than I, if the God whom you worship is pleased with the sacrifice of human life. I consider that God has made me the arbiter of my own fate and all my possibilities. My first duty is to develop all the powers given to me and to make the most of myself and my own life. Self-development is a higher duty than self-sacrifice. I demand the immediate abolition of the Jewish law on vows. Not with my consent can you fulfil yours.[6]

Phyllis Trible has turned her attention precisely to these problematic texts in her *Texts of Terror* (1984).[7] She writes on Hagar, the desolation of rejection; on Tamar, the royal rape of wisdom; on an unnamed woman, the extravagance of violence (the concubine of Judges 19); and the daughter of Jephthah, an inhuman sacrifice. To each of these stories she applies familiar texts but with a twist: '*She* was wounded for our transgressions; *She* was tormented for our iniquities' for Hagar; 'A woman of sorrows and acquainted with grief' for Tamar; 'Her body was broken and given to many' for the unnamed concubine from Bethlehem; and 'My God, my God, why hast thou forsaken her,' for the daughter of Jephthah. She even rewrites the lament of David for Jonathan as a lament for these women and comments, 'Surely words of lament are a seemly offering, for did not the daughters of Israel mourn the daughter of Jephthah every year?' We can get much the same sense of the blighting of young life in Antonia White's novel, *Frost in May* (1933).[8]

In my second chapter I went on to pick out some features of the non-biblical tradition, in order to identify what might still seem to be positively helpful and what has to be repudiated. I pointed out that sexual asceticism *could* be a life-transforming option, free from a measure of male domination, though it could produce

stony asexuality and bizarre behaviour, and could be associated
with the abasement of a woman's visual image so that she would
never appear as a woman in the eyes of a man. Seclusion, and
sexless or male attire were possible defences against misogyny as
well as forms of acceptance of it. Women could be and were
sometimes denigrated and devalued because they were not male,
and they could only approximate to godlikeness in this life
insofar as they approximated to masculinity, became viragos—
when masculinity was associated with spirit and virtue and the
quest for moral and spiritual perfection. I pointed out the
connection of this view with the development of church
structures which would inevitably exclude women, who could be
fairly represented by men, the norm of humanity.

In this chapter I want to turn to a further development of the
tradition, a morbid over-identification with Christ as suffering
victim, connected initially it seems with the clericalization of the
Church stemming from the Gregorian reform of the mid-
eleventh century, and the potentially lethal consequences of this
development for women's spirituality, not least in our own
century. Caroline Bynum has begun to document for us[9] how in
thirteenth- and fourteenth-century piety women who had
flocked into the new religious orders, saw in the eucharist a
central focus of their lives, because whereas only the priest was
authorized to handle the Christ of the rite, it was only in the
eucharist that their desire for direct, almost physical contact with
Christ could receive expression. The feast of Corpus Christi was
fostered by women; religious women had to be forbidden from
communicating constantly—and this at a time when double
monasteries ruled by women as abbesses were virtually eliminated, and when one Bernard of Parma, in a mid-thirteenth century
commentary, was helping to do away with authoritative functions by women: preaching, hearing the confessions of other
nuns, bestowing blessings, touching sacred vessels, veiling and
absolving nuns and so on.[10] This was all during a period—the
thirteenth century—well-known for its renewal of the preferred
male imitation of Christ, that of preacher and evangelist.[11]
Caroline Bynum's work takes us closer to the problems and
strengths of religious women at this time when she turns to her
study of the group known as the nuns of Helfta,[12] who were in
the Benedictine and Cistercian tradition, and the association of

women mystics with the devotion to the wounds, body, blood and heart of Jesus. She has five main points to make at a crucial section in her discussion of the prominence of these women in mysticism.[13] First, they achieved mystical union with a *regal* God, a union she describes as 'controllable, repeatable and coercible', so emphasizing the sacerdotal power of the minister and yet being enabled to transmit that power themselves. Their union with God could be expressed in visions of themselves as priests, which in turn seemed to authorize them to serve as counsellors, mediators and channels to the sacraments. Caroline Bynum properly points out that to be *deprived* of a role depends upon how much that role is valued in a particular period, so mystical union in the context of established monasteries may substitute for clerical status. To this we might venture to add the material cited by Eric Doyle in his essay on the ordination of women in the Roman Catholic Church. Thérèse of Lisieux died at the age of twenty four, the canonical age for ordination at that time, in September 1897, and at the beginning of that year, according to one of her sisters, she had said:

> You see, God is going to take me at an age when I would not have had the time to become a priest ... If I could have been a priest, I would have been ordained at these June ordinations. So, what did God do? So that I would not be disappointed, he let me be sick: in that way I couldn't have been there, and I would die before I could exercise my ministry.

It is said of her that when they cut her hair, she asked for a tonsure, for 'I have a feeling that those who desired to be priests on earth will be able to share in the honour of the priesthood in heaven.'[14]

To return to Caroline Bynum's material and her second point: The eucharistic piety of the nuns whom she studied, not least in their cult of the sacred heart, expressed the same need for direct contact with Christ. 'Although their visions are awash with blood, it is a symbol less of pain and expiation than of nurture and comfort. The dominant note throughout is praise, joy and awareness of glory.'[15] Her third point is that their experience was important for both clergy and laity, who were doubtful about the clericalization of the Church, and their lack of 'power' could make them seem 'purer'. Her fourth point was that their particular form of piety gave them great serenity, and her fifth, that those who grew up within the monastic walls, not least if they were from the nobility, were less likely to be influenced by some views of women propagated outside—as less rational and more lustful. In a sense, these women surpassed the clerical role that they were disqualified from exercising.

Outside those special contexts, however, female piety could and did take a different and pernicious turn, when no such sense of serenity and power was fostered. *If* women were disparaged, they might have a very different understanding of the symbol of a bleeding body with which they desired to be united and which they already represent.[16] My view of this was shaped first of all by my reading of Simone Weil and her appropriation of this deadly form of Christianity. Since my original work on her, I have read and been much interested by Rudolph Bell's recent book *Holy Anorexia,*[17] which is what I think Simone Weil represents in the twentieth century, notwithstanding her other merits. She is a representative of a strand in the tradition that has deep roots in Christian asceticism, piety and the 'imitation of Christ', so far as women can imitate a male saviour. The problem is that whilst in one sense as no-males they cannot be *in persona Christi*, to employ a much over-used and possibly idolatrous phrase, they can be *'in persona Christi'* all too successfully if the Christ they imitate is the dead or dying Christ, rather than the Christ of the resurrection, the regal deity of the Helfta nuns. If they imitate the dying Christ, they may well merit the laments of the 'texts of terror' cited earlier.

Anorexia or lack of appetite as a non-religious phenomenon is found in a number of places in western culture when you start to look for it. In Judith Thurman's biography of Isak Dinesen (Karen Blixen's pen name, which was chosen to recall Isaac, 'the one who laughs', the child of Sarah's old age and divine miracle) one finds that Karen Blixen liked the hardness of edges of living in Africa and that her thinness was her badge of defiance, that fasting for her was an ironic, powerful and essentially feminine act of heroism.[18] Margaret Foster's *Significant Sisters* notices it in the life of Elizabeth Blackwell, the first trained, registered woman doctor,[19] and Roger Poole in his book on Virginia Woolf emphasizes her association of eating with dull minds, sluggish spirits and insensitive souls.[20] Anorexia can then simply function as a means of finding oneself, finding autonomy, finding freedom from anyone or anything that will tell against a girl's or woman's will, what to do, how to do it, or what its value is.

Some religious women are likely rebels against the dependent forms of Christianity on offer to them, and physical asceticism tries to obliterate sexuality as well as hunger and produce a bodily image associated with holiness. Getting control of her body for a girl or woman retrieves her from the sense of helplessness and unbearable inadequacy that she experiences in society and Church by virtue of being female. By means of her asceticism she commands attention, she commands in herself at least at times tremendous energy, and may find what she believes to be communion with God. So she develops techniques to control a self-induced and self-perpetuating system of rewards, and she can then by-pass the religious controls of priests and confessors, those who seem to deny her autonomy. She can become a kind of saviour figure in her own right if she identifies herself with the suffering and dying Christ, for death becomes, so to speak, the only way forward, and death chosen freely and early is still an expression of autonomy, as well as being the only anodyne for a certain kind of pain. Given the Tertullian view that because she is a woman she is somehow personally responsible for Christ's death, she can identify herself as an aggressor,[21] and cope with her anger at this accusation by union with him as a victim. Only in union with Christ can she both maintain her will and feel deeply, intensely connected to divine power, in equality with the male in the privilege of sacrifice in a context in which there is no possibility of effective protest in any other way.

It must be said of course that in western culture it is not just the figure of Christ which may be powerful here. In George Steiner's book on *Antigones* he remarks that

> It is a defining trait of western culture after Jerusalem and after Athens that in it men and women re-enact, more or less consciously, the major gestures, the exemplary symbolic motions, set before them by antique imaginings and formulations. Our realities, as it were, mime the canonic possibilities first expressed in classical art and feeling.[22]

Simone Weil (to whom Steiner does not refer) died in 1943 of failure of the heart muscles following on starvation, tuberculosis and what the coroner called the refusal to eat while the balance of her mind was disturbed;[23] she certainly saw herself as a kind of 'Antigone' figure, the sort of person who could 'take distractedly and as if unconsciously, two or three steps leading to the slippery point where one becomes a prey to gravity and from which one falls on stones that break one's back'.[24] Then, 'There is a certain similarity between the extreme penalty of the cross and that of immuring inflicted on Antigone. This is no doubt due to the same motive—the search for an alibi. One doesn't actually kill; one places the condemned person in a situation in which he or she must necessarily die.'[25] We should connect Simone Weil's perception of herself as 'Antigone' with the feminist perception of Virginia Woolf, and see how not only in her novel *The Years*[26] but in her companion tract, *Three Guineas*, she picks out the Antigone theme to work on, especially Antigone's final confrontation with Creon. She says, ''Tis not my nature to join in hating but in loving', and he replies, 'Pass then, to the world of the dead, and if thou must needs love, love them. While I live, no woman shall rule me.'[27]

With or without 'Antigone', the dangers of the tradition of the imitation of Christ for women are very well illustrated in the work of Karen Armstrong, herself a survivor of 'holy' anorexia as she described in her two volumes of autobiography, *Through the Narrow Gate* and *Beginning the World*.[28] In her recent book, *The Gospel according to Woman*,[29] she quotes a twelfth-century text of masochism and eroticism, which will do for a start. 'Let my body hang with thy body nailed to the cross, enclosed transversely within four walls, and I will hang with thee and never more come down from my cross until I die ... Ah Jesus! sweet it is with thee to hang!'[30] She also cites the profession of the seventeenth-century St Margaret Mary Alacoque, when Jesus says to her, 'all your powers and senses must be buried in Me. You must be deaf, dumb, blind and insensible to all earthly objects.'[31] Karen Armstrong, like the rest of us, has her own battles to fight, but we cannot easily dismiss as deliberately and selectively polemical this kind of material employed in her work when we can also find it in Hans Urs von Balthasar's interpretation of the Carmelite Elizabeth of the Trinity.[32] She died, aged twenty-six, in 1906, and von Balthasar voices no criticism of what he quotes, as for instance when Elizabeth wrote, 'How mysterious and silent is my little cell with its bare walls where hangs a cross of black wood without the body. That is my cross; on it I must sacrifice myself each moment, to be conformed with my crucified bridegroom.' Of Psalm 45.9, 'The queen stands at thy right hand' she makes an expression of the attitude of one who walks on the road to Calvary at the right hand of the crucified and humiliated king.[33]

Such interpretation can of course sustain people in situations of real extremity. For instance, the philosopher Dr Edith Stein had to live those texts out, as it were, as Carmelite Sister Teresa Benedicta of the Cross, who died with her sister, Rose, *not* a convert to Roman Catholicism, when they were taken from the Dutch Carmel, to which Sister Teresa had been moved and where her sister had been given shelter, to Auschwitz in 1942.[34] The point is, however, that the tradition has been lethal for women in circumstances which were by no means as extreme as Auschwitz, and Simone Weil (my main example in this chapter) is as it were on the boundary between them.

Simone Weil has become important in some circles as a kind of World War II (probably unbaptized) saint, and my interest in her here is not in her many merits, but in what helped to bring her to her death. I would not deny that whatever she wrote, whether for her own needs or for publication, is likely to be worth our attention. In particular, she is important for a critique of the egocentrism which infects our culture, and which is at odds with some Christian doctrines of coinherence, and for her unease with mere materialism and her hunger for elements of transcendence. In my view, what helped to bring her and others like her to a premature death were elements of theology from the 'imitation of Christ' tradition. Simone Weil was born and brought up in a terrible Europe, and her life was a constant struggle with affairs over which she could have had no control, not least the slide of her society into totalitarianism. A particular kind of Christianity allied itself with her own problems of self-perception and the constrictions that her society seemed to place around her, and she reached the point when she could not control her body, when her asceticism took her to the point from which there could be no return. What seems astonishing is how the particular kind of Christianity that she represents can still be commended, not least by men, partly because she, as with other women, represents yet another idealization, this time of one who apparently succeeds in the attempt to kill off the 'self' that is

46

supposed to stand in the way of union with God, the death of the self so that true life may begin.[35]

I can accept the criticism that perhaps in her *writings* she had clearly distinguished between morbidity and true spirituality, so that for those who think her death-in-life can be distinguished from her words, she can function as a kind of intellectual and moral 'redemptrix' in the best feminine manner. Alternatively, we can come to see that the totality of her self-annihilation reveals the extremity of the needs which fuel it, needs of nurture and connection, which need to be met in some other way. In Adrienne Rich's poem, 'A Vision: Thinking of Simone Weil' she concludes:

> What is your own will that it
> can so transfix you
> why are you forced to take this test
> over and over and call it God
> why not call it you and get it over
> you with your hatred of enforcement
> and your fear of blinding?[36]

Even Simone Weil seems at the last to have recognized her needs and to have been able to express them, paradoxically when they could no longer be met, because her progress to death was by then irreversible. Among her very last notes as she lay dying she wrote of the alliance between matter and real emotions, of the importance of meals on solemn occasions, of festivals, family reunions, meetings between two friends, when special foods and titbits were so important, signifying the joy of the festival or the meeting.[37] It was that alliance between matter and emotion, which she and others like her have not lived to be able to explore in circumstances which would allow them to do so. Because it is Christian imagery that she and those from whom she learned it have employed, it seems to be very difficult, especially for male critics, to see that the search for meaning and autonomy for women needs to be expressed in a way which does not precipitate them into the process of irreversible self-destruction, however laudable their intentions may seem at first sight. As Joyce Carol Oates has asked, do we so crave 'saintliness' in others, if not in ourselves, that we will transform 'a sick, desperate, broken woman into a model of spiritual health?'[38] What are the grounds on which she asks this question?

Right towards the end of her life, in relative safety in London, Simone Weil wrote a truly appalling prayer along the lines of the material that I quoted earlier, though she did insist to herself that one could not voluntarily demand what the petitions were for, that it was despite oneself, though with consent, entire and without reservation a movement of the whole being. The prayer included petition to the Father to grant her, in the name of Christ,

> That I may be unable to will any bodily movement, or even any attempt at movement, like a total paralytic. That I may be incapable of receiving any sensation, like someone who is completely blind, deaf, and deprived of all the senses. That I may be unable to make the slightest connection between two thoughts...

She asked for will, sensibility, intelligence, love to be stripped away, 'devoured by God, transformed into Christ's substance, and given for food to afflicted men whose body and soul lack every kind of nourishment. And let me be a paralytic—blind, deaf, witless and utterly decrepit.'[39] The afflicted men of whom she wrote—and we should explicitly name the women too—were presumably the dead and dying of the battlefields and cities of two 'world' wars, and of Europe's extermination and concentration camps.

This is just one example of what are monstrous images by which to conceive of the deity's dealings with human creatures, images which, for their violence, are among the most perplexing features of her writing, and which were, in their employment, disastrous for her personality. Sexual violence rightly horrified her,[40] but she found in her horror analogies for the operation of divine grace. The two worst examples are as follows. 'Death and rape—two metaphors for describing the action of the Holy Spirit on the soul. Murder and rape are crimes owing to the fact that they constitute illegitimate imitations of God's actions'.[41] And, 'tearing a girl away from her mother's side, against her will—the greatest and most painful form of violence that it is possible for men to commit—is what serves us as an image of grace'.[42] The moral sensibility that she deployed so effectively in some contexts seems here to have deserted her entirely, but at least there is one point that can be made in her favour. When she wrote her prayer about the sacrificial imitation of the crucified Christ, she followed it with metaphors somewhat comparable with those quoted above. For then she wrote:

> But all these spiritual phenomena are absolutely beyond my competence. I know nothing about it. They are reserved for those who possess, to begin with, the elementary moral virtues. I can only speak of them haphazard. And I cannot even sincerely tell myself that I am speaking haphazard.[43]

Haphazard or not, the metaphors she had learned from a strand of the Christian tradition enabled her to inflict on herself, by accident, the kind of death she might have come to in a concentration camp, so she becomes one of those to whom the 'ghastly verbal witticism *être suicidé*' would have been appropriate.[44] She, with others who have employed these metaphors, becomes then yet another example of someone in whom the creative imagination has atrophied and finally failed: 'the "artist" of suicide is a grasping, blundering, failed artist', whose artwork remains only as a 'mockery of feminine achievement'.[45] The prayer that she wrote, couched in Christian terms though it is, could be seen as analogous to Sylvia Plath's poem 'Lady Lazarus',[46] in which the author writing only a few months before her own suicide in February 1963, wrote to relate her own suffering with those of the tortured Jews of an earlier generation. Her words illuminate the anguish of someone like Simone Weil, without the mask of the 'imitation of Christ' tradition. Part of her poem runs:

> These are my hands
> My knees.
> I may be skin and bone,
>
> Nevertheless I am the same, identical woman.
>   * * *
> Dying
> Is an art, like everything else.
> I do it exceptionally well.
> I do it so it feels like hell.
> I do it so it feels real.
> I guess you could say I've a call.
>   * * *
> For the eyeing of my scars, there is a charge
> For the hearing of my heart—
> It really goes.
>
> And there is a charge, a very large charge
> For a word or a touch
> Or a bit of blood

Or a piece of my hair or my clothes.

The position is complicated for Simone Weil as someone born Jewish but having little sense of it during her own childhood, though as she grew up she learned all too well about Christian anti-Semitism. Her Jewishness could have been a resource for her, since its sense of the celebration of flourishing and fruition could have helped her to free herself from 'the falsity of a near masochism' in her attacks on the falsity of complacency.[47] Her anguish is illuminated by 'Lady Lazarus' in another way, however, in that, like other women influenced by a certain kind of Christianity, she was deeply at odds with herself about her femininity, which may not have been helped by her mother's preference for values associated with little boys rather than little girls, such as forthrightness, though one could hardly criticize her for that in particular.[48] She seems to have been like Lûmir in Claudel's play *Le Pain dur* who says:

> I am not very beautiful. If I were very beautiful, perhaps it would be worth the trouble of living.
> I do not know how to dress.
> I have none of the arts of woman.
> I have always lived like a boy. Nothing but men around me.
> Look how everything hangs on me. It's flung on anyhow.[49]

It was recalled of Simone Weil that 'Her usual costume was a loose, tailored dress of masculine cut, with large side-pockets that were always full of tobacco, worn with the low-heeled shoes of a little girl.'[50] She could and did find a 'religious' justification for what might originally have been no more than the self-image of the revolutionary intelligentsia of her day. 'To accept poverty in the literal sense of the word, as St Francis did, is to accept being nothing in the appearance which one presents to oneself and to others, just as one *is* nothing in reality.'[51] One can see how this language could be deeply damaging to her, rather as in another of Claudel's plays, *L'Annonce faite à Marie*, Violaine says, 'The male is the priest but it is not forbidden to the woman to be a victim.'[52]

Simone Weil also wrote that 'To use the flesh to hide ourselves from the light—is that not a mortal sin? Terrible thought. Better to be a leper.'[53] Claudel, as it happens, expresses what she may have meant in a poem to the lepers of the Hôpital St Louis:

So much the worse for this poor house
If I have destroyed it a bit!
This God with you, this Brother,
You haven't paid too dearly for Him.
I am fire! He who touches Me
Must consent to be burnt.
A victim a living sacrifice,
Do you cease to be My child?
My child, My only child!
And if I took your tunic from you
Of what use was that vesture?[54]

She was notoriously 'touchy' about any physical contact or expression of affection, and her asceticism may well have been one way of trying to get control of her formidable talents and personality in a society which would have been more comfortable for her had she continued to work as a teacher, or at any rate fulfilled some other socially acceptable role. Her determination to push herself to the limits of her endurance was another disastrous trait in a person who apparently took to asceticism so easily, eating all too little and smoking incessantly—a necessary stimulant despite its being the Achilles heel of her asceticism. At least one medical practitioner whom she met in Marseilles seems to have realized that she was ill, and to have recognized a strand in her illness:

I also told Simone a story that I had heard from my sister, the story of a nun who had gone for a very long time without eating. 'She nourished herself on the holy eucharist', my sister had said. Simone found this story quite reasonable.

When I told these stories to Simone, I wasn't very happy with myself. I had the sensation that I was both giving her pleasure and doing her *harm*. That was how it was with this creature who was at war with her own life. If you did one side of her good, you wounded the other side.[55]

Her particular variety of 'holy anorexia' could have been triggered off by her fear of failure, for she herself recounted how at the age of fourteen she fell into a pit of bottomless despair, and seriously thought of dying because of her 'mediocre' abilities— which were to take her to the Ecole Normale Supérieure in 1928 in the same year as Simone de Beauvoir, two women together at the top of their year. She believed herself to be inferior in

51

comparison with her brother, who became a great mathematician. She claimed not to mind visible success, but grieved until she convinced herself that no matter what her natural abilities she could 'penetrate to the kingdom of truth reserved for genius', if only she longed for it and perpetually concentrated her attention upon its attainment.[56] She was to refer to this goal of her life in an all too revealing way when she wrote of

> those beings who have, in spite of flesh and blood, spiritually crossed a boundary equivalent to death, receive on the farther side another life, which is not primarily life, which is primarily truth, truth which has become living, as true as death and as living as life. A life, as Grimm's fairy tales put it, as white as snow and as red as blood. It is that which is the breath of truth, the divine Spirit.[57]

In *The Second Sex* (1949), Simone de Beauvoir hit by chance on an apt commentary on the fairy-tale imagery all too suitable for the sufferer from 'holy anorexia', when she said:

> St Blandine, her white body blood-streaked under the lion's claws, Snow White laid out as if dead in a glass coffin, the Beauty asleep, the fainting Atala, a whole flock of delicate heroines bruised, passive, wounded, kneeling, humiliated, demonstrate to their young sister the fascinating prestige of martyred, deserted, resigned beauty.[58]

Simone Weil might have been able to flourish had she been able to acknowledge, in Doris Lessing's words, that 'all sanity depends on this: that it should be a delight to feel the roughness of a carpet under smooth soles, a delight to feel heat strike the skin, a delight to stand upright, knowing the bones are moving easily under the flesh. If this goes, then the conviction of life goes too.'[59]

It is already clear how Simone Weil would probably have responded to Helen Oppenheimer's argument, which concludes that resurrection is 'the fulfilment in which the pattern of each person shall again become present, our own real presence of which we may each say (perhaps in surprised delight) "This is my body."'[60] Rather, the crucified man-God is a sort of 'reversed image of the white blood-stained martyr' with whom the little girl may have been accustomed to identify herself, except that here a man has assumed or exemplified her role.[61] Whereas one might read the imagery as carrying with it that promise of resurrection, Simone Weil could read it only as a symbol of much longed for peace, free of domination. For she persuaded herself that:

> Those who place their life outside their own bodies are really
> stronger than the rest, who appear to be invulnerable... But fate
> discovers where their life is laid up and deflates them.
>
> The man who places his life in faith in God can lose his faith. But the
> man who places his life in God himself—he will never lose it.
>
> One must place one's life in something one cannot touch on any
> account. It is impossible. It is a death. It means no longer being alive.
> And that is exactly what is wanted.[62]

Had she been in a situation of terrible privation, her asceticism
would have manifested itself as a love dominating the whole
personality, but deprived of such an object of love she became
conscious only of desperate fatigue, and eventually of a total lack
of patience with herself.

> Catholic communion. God has not only made himself flesh once;
> every day he makes himself matter in order to give himself to man
> and be consumed by him. Conversely, through fatigue, affliction,
> death, man is made matter and consumed by God. How refuse this
> reciprocity?'[63]

Exhaustion she understood as 'the mechanism of resignation' to
affliction, killing the desire for deliverance from it,[64] and toyed
with the idea that 'God likes to use castaway objects, waste,
rejects'.[65] After all, 'it does not matter if the consecrated host is
made of the poorest quality flour, not even if it is three parts
rotten'.[66] She expressed her attitude to herself as 'contempt,
hatred and repulsion', and reminded herself of 'My two enemies:
fatigue and *disgust* (physical disgust for all kinds of things). Both of
them well nigh invincible; and under certain circumstances can,
in a flash, make me fall very low.'[67] Sometimes her surroundings
were associated with her depression, and certainly eating became
a chore, since she was disgusted by any food not absolutely
flawless.[68]

For someone who could be extraordinarily perceptive about
herself and others, it was disastrous for her not to recognize her
illness for what it was and to go on judging herself as harshly as
she did and to find 'religious' justification for so doing. 'The
refuge of laziness and inertia, a temptation to which I succumb
very often, almost every day, or I might say every hour, is a
particularly despicable form of consolation. It compels me to
despise myself.'[69] She therefore made use of a particularly

puzzling bit of biblical material, when she confessed that 'I never read the story of the barren fig tree without trembling. I think that it is a portrait of me. In it also, nature was powerless, and yet it was not excused. Christ cursed it ... the sense of being like a barren fig tree for Christ tears my heart.'[70] Again, as she became increasingly self-critical at the limits of her natural strength, 'There are some words in Isaiah which are terrible for me: They that love God "Shall run and not be weary; and they shall walk and not faint." This makes it physically impossible for me to forget, even for a moment, that I am not of their number.'[71]

She wrote a miniature story, found loose among her papers, which should be juxtaposed with her terrible prayer, so that we can see that she was at least aware of resources other than the deadly imagery of the 'imitation of Christ'. She wrote it as though it were about someone else, simply by using the masculine gender, and two thirds of the story give no hint of the emotional 'twist' of the last part, which I will quote separately:

He entered my room and said: 'Poor creature, you who understand nothing, who know nothing. Come with me, and I will teach you things which you do not suspect.' I followed him.

He took me into a church. It was new and ugly. He led me up to the altar and said: 'Kneel down.' I said 'I have not been baptized.' He said 'Fall on your knees before this place, in love, as before the place where lies the truth.' I obeyed.

He brought me out and made me climb up to a garret. Through the open window one could see the whole city spread out, some wooden scaffoldings, and the river on which boats were being unloaded. The garret was empty, except for a table and two chairs. He bade me be seated.

We were alone, He spoke. From time to time someone would enter, mingle in the conversation, then leave again.

Winter had gone; spring had not yet come. The branches of the trees lay bare, without buds, in the cold air full of sunshine.

The light of day would arise, shine forth in splendour, and fade away; then the moon and the stars would enter through the window. And then once more the dawn would come up.

At times he would fall silent, take some bread from a cupboard, and we would share it. This bread really had the taste of bread. I have never found that taste again.

54

He would pour out some wine for me, and some for himself—wine which tasted of the sun and of the soil upon which this city was built.

At other times we would stretch ourselves out on the floor of the garret, and sweet sleep would enfold me. Then I would wake and drink in the light of the sun.

He had promised to teach me, but he did not teach me anything. We talked about all kinds of things, in a desultory way, as do old friends.[72]

This may be regarded as her attempt in prose to re-express Herbert's poem 'Love', which she used as a prayer, albeit unintentionally to begin with.[73] Of the problems to do with the reading of this poem, it is perhaps worth drawing attention here to the one that surfaces in Amanda Cross's novel, *Death in a Tenured Position*, which relates the death in Harvard of a woman professor, a distinguished interpreter of the works of George Herbert. In this novel Kate Fansler says of the suicide of her friend Janet that it had something to do with the way in which she read this poem. The poem, she says, 'speaks for a man who considers himself unworthy in his life and religion, being urged to sit down with Christ and be served by him . . . What eventually occurred to me is that it could be read as an invitation to death, that one was ready to join Christ in heaven, to get there, furthermore, by eating. Eating death, perhaps . . .' She concludes that 'I like to think she died believing that she had been called to a holy feast, but I don't believe it. That kind of faith belonged to Herbert's time, and Herbert's sort. I want to believe she believed, for my own sake.'[74]

Simone Weil certainly was tormented by a sense of unworthiness, for she thought that so far as other people were concerned, there was a sense in which she did not exist for them. 'I am the colour of dead leaves, like certain insects which go unnoticed',[75] and, 'I am not the girl who is waiting for her lover, but the tiresome third party who is sitting with two lovers and has got to get up and go away if they are to be really together.'[76] Not surprising then, is the 'reversal' of the last third of her garret story:

One day he said to me: 'Now go.' I fell down before him, I clasped his knees, I implored him not to drive me away. But he threw me out on the stairs. I went down unconscious of anything, my heart as it were in shreds. I wandered along the streets. Then I realized that I had no idea where this house lay.

55

I have never tried to find it again. I understood that he had come for me by mistake. My place is not in that garret. It can be anywhere—in a prison cell, in one of those middle-class drawing rooms full of knick-knacks and red plush, in the waiting room of a station—anywhere, except in that garret.

Sometimes I cannot help trying, fearfully and remorsefully, to repeat to myself a part of what he said to me. How am I to know if I remember rightly? He is not there to tell me.

I know well that he does not love me. How could he love me? And yet deep down within me something, a particle of myself, cannot help thinking, with fear and trembling, that perhaps, in spite of all, he loves me.

We might say that one constructive point that she seems to have learned from her longing for and experience of affection was that it provided her with clues for the use of its language in theology, especially 'the smile on a beloved face',[77] 'the love that irradiates the tenderest smile of some body one loves',[78] which was the nearest analogy she could find for her own experiences of a Christ present to her. It was to this clue, and to others of which she was aware: the bread which 'really had the taste of bread', the wine 'which tasted of the sun and of the soil', to which she might have trusted; and she was deeply appreciative of the beauty of the world, a beauty which she saw as the creative gift of God's Son.[79]

> The beauty of the world is Christ's tender smile for us coming through matter. He is really present in the universal beauty. The love of this beauty proceeds from God dwelling in our soul and goes out to God present in the universe. It also is like a sacrament.[80]

Such joy could then have become *joie de vivre* as she herself indicated when she began to develop a sacramental view of work. For example, 'What is required is that this world and the world beyond, in their double beauty, should be present and associated in the act of work, like the child about to be born in the making of the layette.'[81]

It was, however, to be a tragedy that experience and imagery, which offered the possibility not merely of survival but of hope and fulfilment, were in no way as powerful as the alternatives, which had bitten all too deeply into her intellect and emotion, corroding her vitality especially at the time when she was to become adrift briefly in North America and then in war-time Britain, in alien cultures in which her role was anything but clear, or even promising, and our own 'worst-case scenario' culture can seem almost as alien and as threatening to women as hers was to her. Without her fascination with particular and potentially lethal elements of the Christian tradition, she might have survived to become an even greater political philosopher than indeed she was, with her exceptional independence and clarity of mind, generosity and courage harnessed to complete maturity. It was the alliance between matter and emotion that she was unable to explore, and which might have put the elements of Christianity that she did explore into perspective, and thus discover their possible appropriate meaning. It is one thing to employ the metaphors of the 'imitation of Christ' as the context of love and then be sustained by it in a situation of extremity, but quite another to make the bare possibility of being in that situation a focus of attention outside the context of love. Without that context life may be eaten away by metaphor, with those who employ it literally tested to destruction by it. Of the 'imitation of Christ' tradition as it can sometimes be lived and died, I would want to say that it may be the last kind of Christianity that women are likely to need. I would apply to much of it some words from Jacques Pohier's *God in Fragments*:

> What is new is for believers to discover that fidelity is like all the other great human values; one can grow oneself and make others grow by serving them, but one can also degrade and destroy oneself and degrade and destroy others by being enslaved to certain forms of fidelity, just as one can do the same thing by being enslaved to certain figures of justice, truth . . . and even faith. After all, religious faith has produced as many corpses or petrified at least as many living dead as any other great human value.[82]

Notes

1   Immanuel Kant, *Critique of practical reason*, etc., tr. T. K. Abbott (Longmans 1967), p. 25.
2   Immanuel Kant, *Religion within the Limits of Reason Alone*, tr. T. M. Greene and H. H. Hudson (New York, Harper & Row, 1960), p. 77.
3   Iris Murdoch, *Henry and Cato* (Penguin 1983).
4   Cady Stanton, *The Woman's Bible*, p. 67.

5   ibid., part 2, pp. 24–7.
6   ibid., pp. 25–6.
7   Phyllis Trible, *Texts of Terror: Literary Feminist Readings of Biblical Narratives* (Philadelphia, Fortress Press, 1984).
8   Antonia White, *Frost in May* (Fontana/Virago 1982).
9   Caroline Walker Bynum, *Jesus as Mother: Studies in the Spirituality of the High Middle Ages* (California University Press 1982).
10   ibid., pp. 15–16.
11   See Edward Tracy Brett, *Humbert of the Romans: His Life and Views of Thirteenth-Century Society* (Toronto, Pontifical Institute of Mediaeval Studies, 1984).
12   Bynum, *Jesus as Mother*, pp. 170f.
13   ibid., p. 184.
14   Eric Doyle, 'The Ordination of Women in the Roman Catholic Church' in Monica Furlong (ed.), *Feminine in the Church* (SPCK 1984), pp. 28–43, esp. p. 40.
15   Bynum, *Jesus as Mother*, p. 254.
16   See also the essay of Dr Helen King, 'Sacrificial Blood: The Role of the Amnion in Ancient Gynecology' in *Helios* 13 (1986), 'Women in Antiquity' (special issue), part of her conclusion: 'Sacrifice defines the human condition and, within humanity, distinguishes between the sexes. The entry into marriage, the *telos* of the female life, recalls the preparation of a beast for sacrifice: the healthy woman is defined as she who bleeds like a sacrificial victim, in both menstruation and childbirth.'
17   Rudolph M. Bell, *Holy Anorexia* (Chicago University Press 1985); in addition to her *Jesus as Mother*, see Caroline Walker Bynum's 'Women Mystics and Eucharistic Devotion in the Thirteenth Century' in *Women's Studies*, 11 (1984), pp. 179–214.
18   Judith Thurman, *Isak Dinesen: The Life of Karen Blixen* (Penguin 1982), pp. 50, 70.
19   Forster, *Significant Sisters*, p. 63.
20   Roger Poole, *The Unknown Virginia Woolf* (Harvester 1982), pp. 54f.
21   Carl A. Mounteer, 'Guilt, Martyrdom and Monasticism' in *Journal of Psychohistory*, 9:2 (1981), pp. 145–71.
22   George Steiner, *Antigones: The Antigone Myth in Western Literature, Art and Culture* (Clarendon Press 1986), p. 108.
23   Simone Pétrement, *Simone Weil: A Life*, tr. R. Rosenthal (Mowbrays 1976), p. 537.
24   Simone Weil, *Intimations of Christianity among the Greeks*, tr. E. C. Geissbühler (Routledge & Kegan Paul 1976), p. 183.
25   Simone Weil, The Notebooks, 2 vols, tr. A. Wills (Routledge & Kegan Paul 1976), pp. 517–8. See also Simone Weil, *First and Last Notebooks*, tr. R. Rees (Oxford University Press 1970), p. 250: 'Osiris was not only killed but tortured. He was enclosed in a coffin where he died by suffocation, slowly and in terror. Antigone's death was of the same kind.'
26   Virginia Woolf, *The Years* (Granada 1982), pp. 104–6.
27   Virginia Woolf, *Three Guineas* (Hogarth Press 1986), p. 190, n. 40.

See the whole dialogue in Sophocles, *The Theban Plays*, tr. E. F. Watling (Penguin 1974), pp. 138–40.

28   Karen Armstrong, *Through the Narrow Gate* (Pan 1981); *Beginning the World* (Pan 1983).

29   Karen Armstrong, *The Gospel according to Woman* (Elm Tree Books 1986).

30   ibid., p. 151.

31   ibid., p. 154.

32   Hans Urs von Balthasar, *Elizabeth of Dijon: An Interpretation of her Spiritual Mission*, tr. A. V. Littledale (Harvill 1956).

33   ibid., pp. 102–3.

34   James Baade, 'Witness to the Cross' in *The Tablet* (14 April 1984), pp. 355–7.

35   Eric O. Springstead, *Simone Weil and the Suffering of Love* (Cambridge, Mass.; Cowley, 1986), pp. 79f.

36   Adrienne Rich, *A Wild Patience has Taken Me this Far* (New York, W. W. Norton, 1981), p. 50.

37   Weil, *First and Last*, p. 368.

38   '"May God Grant that I Become Nothing": The Mysticism of Simone Weil' in Joyce Carol Oates, *The Profane Art: Essays and Review* (New York, Dutton, 1983), pp. 147–58, esp. p. 158.

39   The full text is quoted in Springstead, op. cit., pp. 80–1.

40   Pétrement, *Simone Weil*, pp. 192–4.

41   Weil, *Notebooks*, p. 390.

42   ibid., p. 401.

42   Weil, *First and Last*, p. 245.

44   David Daube, 'The Linguistics of Suicide' in *Philosophy and Public Affairs*, 1:4 (1972), pp. 367–437, esp. p. 389.

45   Joyce Carol Oates, 'The Art of Suicide' in M. Pabst Battin and D. J. Mayo (eds.), *Suicide, the Philosophical Issues* (New York, St Martin's Press, 1980), p. 162.

46   Sylvia Plath, *Ariel* (Faber & Faber 1965), p. 16–19.

47   Helen Oppenheimer, 'Christian Flourishing' in *Religious Studies*, 5 (1969), pp. 163–71, esp. p. 170.

48   Pétrement, *Simone Weil*, p. 278.

49   E. Beaumont, *The Theme of Beatrice in the Plays of Claudel* (Rockcliff 1954), p. 86.

50   J. Cabaud, *Simone Weil: A Fellowship in Love* (Harvill 1964), p. 32.

51   Weil, *Intimations*, p. 175.

52   P. Claudel, *L'Annonce faite|à Marie* (Paris, Gallimard, 1940), p. 124.

53   Weil, *Notebooks*, p. 623.

54   K. O'Flaherty, *Paul Claudel and 'The Tidings Brought to Mary'* (Basil Blackwell 1948), p. 75.

55   Pétrement, *Simone Weil*, p. 420.

56   Simone Weil, *Waiting on God*, tr. E. Crauford (Fontana 1974), p. 30. See also Simone Weil, *Seventy letters*, tr. R. Rees (Oxford University Press 1965), p. 140.

57 Simone Weil, *The Need for Roots*, tr. A. F. Wills (Routledge & Kegan Paul 1978), p. 328; and see *Notebooks*, p. 583.
58 Simone de Beauvoir, *The Second Sex*, tr. H. M. Parshley (Penguin 1984), p. 319.
59 Doris Lessing, *The Golden Notebook* (Granada 1981), p. 591.
60 Helen Oppenheimer, 'Life After Death' in *Theology*, 82 (1979), pp. 328–35.
61 de Beauvoir, *The Second Sex*, p. 686.
62 Weil, *Notebooks*, pp. 493–4.
63 ibid., p. 99.
64 ibid., p. 140.
65 Weil, *Waiting*, p. 39.
66 Weil, *Seventy Letters*, p. 139.
67 Weil, *Notebooks*, p. 153.
68 Pétrement, *Simone Weil*, p. 81.
69 Weil, *Seventy Letters*, p. 142.
70 Weil, *Waiting*, p. 64.
71 Weil, *Seventy Letters*, p. 170.
72 Weil, *Notebooks*, p. 638.
73 Weil, *Seventy Letters*, p. 142.
74 Amanda Cross, *Death in a Tenured Position* (New York, Ballantine, 1981), pp. 155–6.
75 Weil, *Waiting*, p. 64.
76 Weil, *Notebooks*, p. 404.
77 Weil, *Waiting*, p. 35.
78 Weil, *Seventy Letters*, p. 140.
79 Weil, *Intimations*, pp. 101–4.
80 Weil, *Waiting on God*, p. 120.
81 Weil, *Need for Roots*, p. 91.
82 Jacques Pohier, *God in Fragments*, tr. John Bowden (SCM Press 1985), p. 183.

4

MARTHA'S CONFESSION

Finding a voice in the Christian community

There are two Martha stories in the Gospels, one of which is about the Martha who is *anxious* about many things rather than seizing the priceless opportunity offered to women in discipleship of Jesus. Even with that implicit criticism of her in the text, Martha has always had a fairly good press in church tradition, where the value of the 'active' life and the proper diaconate and service of others are appreciated.[1] She can be a problematical model too, however, as Nancy Ore, an American seminary student, discovered and expressed in her piece, 'You are enough'. After father, mother, husband and children have told her why whatever she does for them is not enough, we have:

It is not enough
said her pastor
that you
     teach the second graders
     change the cloths and candles
     kneel prostrate at the altar
as long as there are starving children in the world
you must
not eat
without guilt.

Her counsellor concludes his advice with the words that she must not feel that she is not enough, at which point she gives up to wait for death. A voice is heard saying 'YOU ARE ENOUGH':

naked
crying
bleeding
nameless
starving
sinful

and only this voice makes possible her 'third day' rising and feasting.[2] This view of a Martha in the third Gospel needs balancing up by the other Martha of the Fourth Gospel, the one who confesses to Jesus, 'You are the Christ, the Son of God, who has come into the world'. It is functionally parallel to Peter's confession of Christ in Mark's and Matthew's Gospels, a confession not uncommonly held to confer apostolic authority on the one who utters it. Martha as disciple here seems not to be in the habit of keeping silence, since in her extremity of need she still finds the energy not only to make her acknowledgement of Christ's authority and its source, but to argue it out with him about her brother Lazarus. There is another example in the Gospels of Jesus made known to a woman, and by her to us also, in a scene of painful human interaction; this is the encounter of Jesus with the Syro-Phoenician woman, a Gentile. Sharon H. Ringe's recent exegesis[3] of this incident makes us confront the strangeness and offensiveness of this story, remembered because it tells us something about Jesus which has not been said elsewhere. For the sake of her beloved daughter, the Syro-Phoenician woman went straight for what she needed, bested Jesus in an argument, and by her wit made possible his ministry to her and to her child. Other women who found their voices in the early Christian communities are represented too by the Samaritan woman of the Fourth Gospel, missionary despite her past; Mary of Magdala; Phoebe the deacon and 'protectress' of Paul and others; Junia, given apostolic acknowledgement by him; and Prisca, who with her husband was described by Paul as a fellow-worker, and many more.[4] Christian mission has, from the beginnings of the movement associated with Jesus of Nazareth, depended upon the commitment of women as well as of men. How then did it come about that it was supposed that women could not have a voice, not even in their own affairs, let alone in the ecclesiastical context?

The answer to this question has to do with the *use* to which certain biblical texts were put, texts which reflect the situation in *some*, but not all, of the communities whose life and problems are reflected in the 'Pauline' letters. These texts have to be seen in their divergence from, as well as sometimes convergence with, the sort of material referred to in my previous paragraph, material to be found also in the original documents of the apostolic age, which contain other expressions of women's roles and possibilities. I make no attempt here to describe what has been done to engage with the exegesis of the particular texts which contain injunctions about women's silence, but would like only to point out that Paul's discussion of what women may put on their heads and why need not be as big a problem as it may first seem. Strictly speaking Paul may not even be referring to 'veiling' women, but to the arrangement of their hair in such a way as not to obscure their femininity.[5] Professor Morna Hooker's explanation of 1 Corinthians 11.2f is that women *were* taking part in prayer and prophecy.[6] The woman has 'authority' on her head to do so; she, like the man, being under the authority of God, with the 'angels' concerned about seeing that worship was conducted in a fitting manner. Both men and women are interdependent in their distinctiveness, not least in the worship of the God who released them from the restrictions of the past. It is not at all clear that it is *Paul*, rather than his interpreters, who needs rescuing from disastrous compromise with religious and social convention, and from habits of exegesis such as can be found in some of the writings of the early Fathers.[7]

There remains, however, the fact that this text too has been used in certain contexts to keep women silent, which means that Paul does not exactly have high 'street credibility' with feminists, any more than do the authors and representatives of other destructive views of women's capabilities in some Christian communities in the past and in the present. It seems to me important to understand the use to which these texts have been put, if we are ever going to address ourselves in sensitive and intelligent ways to the question of the kind of authority which is in the Churches *gratefully* and *gracefully* to be conceded to women, and the form that its expression should take, since women are profoundly bored with the complementary-but-of-course-always-subordinate roles sometimes grudgingly allowed them. It is not now fortunately just a matter for the Churches, though it seems to me that they must carry a great weight of responsibility in the past for the way women have been regarded. But for them in particular, Janet Morley's questions are again pertinent.[8]

Looking at the list of the lesser saints in the Church of England's Alternative Services Book, Janet Morley comments that it is inherently improbable that one sex, the male sex, should be nearly seven times as saintly as the other, a balance which would be startling if the preponderance were the other way. She is therefore right to ask why it is that saintly women are less remembered or deemed to be less important. Moreover, a group of the men, slightly larger than the whole group of the saintly women put together, are distinguished as teachers of the faith (not, since it is the ASB, Catherine of Siena or Theresa of Avila, accorded this distinction in the Roman Catholic Church in 1970, though they are the only two women so honoured). So, once more to use her questions, why is there so much caution in giving women authoritative status? One reason at least is the use of the texts that women were to learn in silence and not to teach or have authority over men, though no doubt we should be grateful that they were permitted to learn.

The person who did more than anyone else to clarify the troublesome use in her White Anglo-Saxon Protestant culture of selective and uncontextualized quotation from Pauline Epistles that had helped to bring women to the pass in which they were was Virginia Woolf. She is known not only for her novels but for her witty feminist essay *A Room of One's Own*, written for university women in Cambridge[9] and first published in 1929,[10] an essay which analyses the social and economic disabilities of women.[11] For those with her particular talents, to have the privacy and freedom to write was essential, obviously, for publication in her own right, under her own name; what she needed was a room of her own, with a door that she could shut against those who for ever wanted her to be at their disposal rather than at her own. She could be said to begin the movement sometimes indicated by the phrase 'Thinking back through our mothers', with her question about what our mothers had been doing that they had no wealth to leave to their daughters? 'Powdering their noses? Looking in at shop windows? Flaunting in the sun at Monte Carlo?' Mother, she tells us, may have been a wastrel in her spare time (after bearing thirteen children by a minister of the Church), but if so, 'her gay and dissipated life had left too few traces of its pleasures on her face'. So here was one answer: 'Making a fortune and bearing thirteen children—no human being could stand it.'[12] She tried to hunt out answers to questions such as 'Why did men drink wine and women water?' and 'Why was one sex so prosperous and the other so poor?' And in tackling the literature on women written by men, she asked herself why the men seemed to be so angry. Because, she says, they were protesting against some infringement of their power to believe in themselves. She decided that women have served all

64

these centuries as looking-glasses, possessing the magic and delicious power of reflecting the figure of man at twice its natural size. 'How is he to go on giving judgement, civilizing natives, making laws, writing books, dressing up and speechifying at banquets, unless he can see himself at breakfast and dinner at least twice the size he really is?'[13] (It is this idea, incidentally, that Mary Daly picks up and develops in her concluding pages of *Beyond God the Father* on the 'Looking Glass' society.)[14] Virginia Woolf gives us an example of the way in which the 'mirroring' works in *The Years* (1937), when she wrote of a doctor, Peggy, at a party, feeling the skin around her lips and eyes tight from the tiredness of sitting up late with a woman in childbirth. A young man talks to her:

> Her attention wandered. She had heard it all before. I, I, I—he went on. It was like a vulture's beak pecking, or a vacuum-cleaner sucking, or a telephone bell ringing. I, I, I. But he couldn't help it . . . He could not free himself, could not detach himself . . .

> 'I'm tired,' she apologized. 'I've been up all night,' she explained. 'I'm a doctor—' The fire went out of his face when she said 'I'. That's done it—now he'll go, she thought. He can't be 'you'—he must be 'I'. She smiled. For up he got and off he went.[15]

Virginia Woolf gained little from the material available to her. It seemed to be an odd monster that one could make up by reading the historians first and the poets afterwards: 'a worm winged like an eagle; the spirit of life and beauty in a kitchen chopping up suet'.[16] She herself tried to imagine a sister for Shakespeare, though she thought that being thwarted and hindered by others, tortured and pulled asunder by her own contrary instincts, she must have lost her health and sanity. The problem was that chastity had then, 'it has even now a religious importance in a woman's life',[17] so wrapped around with nerves and instincts that to cut it free and bring it to the light of day demanded rare courage. 'It was the relic of the sense of chastity that dictated anonymity to women even as late as the nineteenth century'— women sought ineffectively 'to veil themselves by using the name of a man'.

Thus they did homage to the convention that publicity in women is detestable '(the chief glory of a woman is not to be talked of, said Pericles, himself a much-talked of man)', that anonymity runs in their blood, that the desire to be veiled still possesses them. 'They are not even now as concerned about the health of their fame as men are, and, speaking generally, will pass a tombstone or a signpost without feeling an irresistible desire to cut their names on it.' The imperial spirit being what it was, she added that 'It is one of the great advantages of being a woman that one can pass even a very fine negress without wishing to make an Englishwoman of her'.[18]

Virginia Woolf was indeed fascinated by that profoundly interesting subject, the value that men set upon women's chastity and its effect upon their education. In *Three Guineas*, published in 1938 and recently reprinted,[19] she was perceptive about the difference between the money paid for centuries into the AEF—Arthur's Education Fund—and that expensive item in the bourgeois budget,[20] the protection of a woman's chastity by maids, putting into practice the commands of the Pauline letters, and doing her utmost to deliver her mistress's body intact to her master. Paul's words about the need for women to be veiled during prayer and prophecy had been invoked to prevent women from studying medicine, painting in the nude, reading Shakespeare and playing in orchestras, as well as from walking down Bond Street alone.[21] Virginia Woolf may have been particularly sensitive to women's problems in the public performance of music from her friendship with Dame Ethel Smyth, who published lectures on women and music in *Female Pipings in Eden* (1934).[22] Dame Ethel had said that men's 'vicarious sense of modesty' had kept women from playing the cello but allowed her to play the 'unlucrative harp', the men cherishing her 'white-armed presence in their midst, much as the men in the Welsh regiment cherish the regimental goat'.[23] She knew that you could not have Mont Blanc and Mount Everest without the moderate-sized mountains on whose shoulders they stand. 'We know what "Candide" said about the duty of cultivating your garden; but what if the authorities keep all the agricultural instruments under lock and key?'[24] If, she said, from the very first Eve had been granted a chance of self-development, 'there would have been no furtive hanging about the Tree of Knowledge, no illicit truck with serpents and apples, and of course—this would have been rather sad—no Militant Suffragettes.'[25]

It was one thing for Virginia Woolf to identify some of the sources of women's difficulties, but quite another to overcome them, and not least the problem of how women are to come to take responsibility for themselves. In a famous passage from a speech of 1931 called 'The Death of the Moth' she talked of how she had to kill in herself 'the angel in the house', her symbol of female collusion in subjection now more familiar to us. The 'angel' was intensely sympathetic, immensely charming, utterly unselfish. She excelled herself in the difficult arts of family life, sacrificing herself daily.

> If there was a chicken, she took the leg; if there was a draught, she sat in it—in short she was so constituted that she never had a mind or a wish of her own, but preferred to sympathise always with the minds and wishes of others. Above all—I need not say it—she was pure.[26]

The problems of the 'angel' are now receiving more attention, not least by people concerned with pastoral theology, who have written of the sins of self-negation, of triviality, distractibility, diffusiveness, lack of an organizing centre, dependence on others for self-definition, all more likely perhaps to be characteristic of women rather than of men.[27]

Virginia Woolf is primarily concerned with the resurgence as well as rediscovery of writing by women, and less likely to concern herself with what had been done to find women a voice in religious contexts, using the resources of Scripture. We could cite here the Quaker Margaret Fell, for instance, who in 1666 had produced *Women's speaking justified, proved and allowed of by the Scriptures*[28] (recently back in print), and the magnificent Mary Ward, the Roman Catholic who died in 1645 having pioneered active *un*enclosed congregations for women, on the model of the Society of Jesus. Interested in the Society's educational methods, with a graduated order of studies correlated with the capacities of their pupils, she wanted not only to found boarding schools for 'ladies' but to teach poor girls, a project not previously tackled by women living in community. Not welcomed by the Jesuits, her self-chosen association with them itself provoked opposition in a society which deemed them to be the political agents of a hostile papacy. She wanted her Institute to be unenclosed, so as to be able to gain access to where poor girls lived, and to modify her dress and that of her companions according to circumstances, varying between the dress of her social class when travelling and living back in England, and a modified 'religious' dress on the

67

Continent of Europe.[29] Her Institute was suppressed in 1631 after complaints that apart from exposing themselves to secular society, women in her company 'presume and arrogate to themselves authority to speak about spiritual things before grave men and even sometimes when priests are present to hold exhortation in an assembly of Catholics'.[30] The actual bull of suppression charged that they 'under the guise of promoting the salvation of souls, have been accustomed to attempt and to employ themselves at many other works which are most unsuited to their weak sex and character, to female modesty and particularly to maidenly reserve'. Not until 1909 were the members of the Institute of the Blessed Virgin Mary allowed to describe Mary Ward as their foundress, by which time the Institute included seventy thousand girls in its schools.

One must here recall that during the Renaissance there had been some remarkable discussions of women's nature which to some extent had modified the proscriptions about what was and was not permitted to women. Not the least astonishing of these discussions was the early sixteenth-century treatise 'On the Nobility and Excellence of Women', by Aggrippa von Nettesheim.[31] For our present theme, it is entertaining to note his defence of women's talkativeness, women being better spoken, more eloquent, copious and plentiful of words than a man,—as Linda Woodbridge comments, 'a logical extension of the humanist glorification of speech as a distinctive attribute of mankind',[32] and which in this particular case connects nicely with Aggrippa von Nettesheim's observations that Eve was God's last and hence highest creation. His fundamental argument is one for equality:

> The only difference between man and woman is physical... In everything else they are the same. Woman does not have a soul of a different sex from that which animates man. Both received a soul which is absolutely the same and of an equal condition. Women and men were equally endowed with the gifts of spirit, reason, and the use of words; they were created for the same end, and the sexual difference between them will not confer a different destiny...[33]

The most shocking argument he advances, however, is that Christ would have become female in the Incarnation, were it not for the need to deal with male pride:

> Wishing to take on human nature in its lowest and most abject state, so as the more effectively by this humiliation to expiate the first

68

man's pride of sinning, Jesus Christ chose the male sex as the more despicable, not the female, who is nobler and more regenerate than the male. Moreover, because the human species was driven to evil doing more by the sin of man than that of woman, God wanted the sin to be expiated in the sex that had sinned, whereas he wanted the sex which had been taken by surprise and tricked to bring forth Him in whom the sin was to be revenged.

Linda Woodbridge thus pinpoints precisely Aggrippa von Nettes-heim's real target, which is not the outright misogynist but (more difficult to deal with) male lovers of women, who are at the same time male supremacists and who indulge themselves in well-intentioned paternalism. This lends weight to his and anyone else's attention to 'great women in history': 'women have done more in the past than they are doing now, because contemporary society denies them the education and the legal rights they must have to perform what they are capable of'.[34] Quite without benefit of Aggrippa von Nettesheim, however, there is a remarkable example of the work of one such woman from the medieval period, which turned up in Virginia Woolf's own day (the nearest approximation to an ancestress for Shakespeare or a sister for Chaucer we are likely to find). It is Margery Kempe's *Book*;[35] which is not the product of the religious houses or schools, which still fostered some of the educated women of the Middle Ages. Rather, it is the work of a vigorous, determined and courageous laywoman, who had to have help, perhaps from one of her sons in the first place, both for the first draft of her book and then for the book as we now have it, revised probably in 1436, so far as the first part is concerned, and then completed after her trip to Germany in 1438. This first English autobiography is a book about one woman's religious experience, and a woman, moreover, who had found her voice and who could not be silenced. Reflected in it is the England of Henry IV, V and VI, as well as her own dilemmas and those of the religious and secular priests who supported her. Copied perhaps once, one complete text survived in the collection of the Carthusians of Mount Grace, one of whom also had the temerity to translate into Latin Marguerite Porete's *Mirror of Simple Souls*, for which she had been burned in Paris in 1310.[36] Margery Kempe's *Book* was passed to a recusant family, whose descendants had tucked it into a library shelf, until in 1934 its owner showed it to the distinguished American medievalist Miss Hope Emily Allen. It was then published with her notes, in an edition by Professor Sanford Brown Meech in 1940. This book, known earlier only by short and misleading excerpts (and in complete contrast to the *Showings* of Dame Julian of Norwich, whom Margery Kempe visited) is as close as we are ever likely to get to the life and religious experiences of an outstandingly tough and lively woman, without her experiences being over-controlled by the male representatives of the ecclesiastical institutions of her day, though a priest-friend produced the final draft for her. Only as a result of recent research, however, is it possible to place her, after forty years, more accurately than ever before, in the tradition which is now coming alive, of a whole group of medieval women known both by name and by their written theology and spirituality. We can identify the way in which she expresses herself in relation to women in the religious movements which were proving so attractive to women on the Continent—both the establishment of new orders which could offer new vocations to women, and the looser, self-regulating communities of women to be found, particularly in the Netherlands. There may have been hundreds of women like her.

Margery Kempe has had a relatively bad press from writers on spirituality, since they seem to want to fit her into a mould which cannot accommodate her. Dom David Knowles was a particularly severe critic, who employed the same criteria of 'perfection' to her as to writers of some of the classics of English mystical writing.[37] To give a more recent example of the sort of criticism that still bedevils our understanding of her, we might take Simon Tugwell's *Ways of Imperfection*,[38] in which he seems puzzled by the fact that Margery Kempe, married at the age of twenty in 1393 or 1394, coped with her particular sense of vocation by taking a vow of chastity, to which she had to persuade her husband to agree. This her husband eventually did, on Midsummer Eve (probably 23 June 1413) as they were coming from York 'in right hot weather', she carrying a bottle of beer in her hand, and her husband a cake tucked inside his clothes against his chest. Tugwell writes that the beginning of Margery's religious experiences coincides with 'a violent and apparently sudden distaste for lying with her husband'.[39] But Tugwell fails to tell us what is clear from the text, that by this time Margery had borne fourteen children (presumably fourteen pregnancies resulting in children born alive, though she does not tell us how many survived their first, fifth or fifteenth years). She had a very difficult first pregnancy and suffered from some form of what would now be called post-natal psychosis for the best part of a year afterwards, from which she believed Christ himself had delivered her[40]—the first of her religious experiences—and which made her both profoundly compassionate and effective in helping another woman in a similar state.[41] The suffering associated with pregnancy may well have had something to do with her need to take the vow. Furthermore, there is no point in misunderstanding her experience and denigrating her devotion to the Virgin and the Holy Family, hardly untypical of the men and women of her age,[42] unless it is to dismiss the importance of some of the claims that she is making for herself and for other women too.

The deal that Margery Kempe struck with her husband included her agreement to eat with him on Fridays and to pay off his debts, in return for a joint vow of chastity, and she was fortunate in having some financial resources of her own when her father died. It is worth recalling too that she is living in a society some of whose members still maintained the values of Jerome's sexual score card, with virginity rating one hundred points, widowhood sixty and marriage thirty. So to take a vow of chastity and approximate to widowhood was to enable her to pursue union with the Christ who authorized it, though she did return to her husband to nurse him through his final years. By her vow she was free not only to travel from her home in King's Lynn over England, but also to go on pilgrimage, to the Holy Land as well as to Compostella. She was, of course, deeply dependent on her clerical friends for her instruction by sermons and for her knowledge of Scripture and of writers on prayer, as well as for their evaluation of her religious experiences. It could be argued that in many ways her clerical friends had done her proud, and she in turn had, on the whole, good and generous friendships with them. She seems to have suffered more from the laity of her day than from religious and clerics; and she had the courage to criticise her ecclesiastical superiors, for she rebuked the Archbishop of Canterbury for allowing his retainers to swear and the Bishop of Lincoln for placing human respect before the love of God. They in turn came to respect her.

She was of course sometimes in real physical danger, for her own parish priest, William Sawtre, went to the stake in 1401 for being a 'Lollard'[43] (a contemptuous label meaning mumbler, a follower of Wyclif), and in Henry V's day a preacher, John Swetstock, denounced those who asked why women should not be priested and enabled to celebrate and preach like men.[44] Lollardy was to be associated especially with family religion and the transmission of religious teaching by women.[45] She clearly was not a Lollard, for they did not characteristically fast, go on pilgrimages, frequent confession, attend the eucharist frequently, or attach as much importance to religious art as she did.[46] But it is important to bear this background in mind when we look at just one example from her *Book*, her encounter with Henry Bowet, Archbishop of York, at Cawood, seven miles from York, in 1417.[47] When she was brought to the Archbishop's chapel many of his household despised her, calling her 'loller' and 'heretic', and they swore 'many a horrible oath' that she should be burned. Through the strength of Jesus, as she put it, she replied to them, 'Sirs, I fear me that you shall be burned in hell without end unless you amend yourselves of your oath swearing, for you keep not the commandments of God. I would not swear as you do for all the good of this world.' When she was brought before the Archbishop himself, he found that she knew her Articles of Faith, and after giving him as good as she got in a very comic exchange between the two of them, he said to her, 'Thou shalt swear that thou shalt neither teach nor challenge the people in my diocese.' Her reply was, 'Nay, sir, I shall not swear', for:

> I shall speak of God and reprove those that swear great oaths wheresoever I go unto the time that the pope and Holy Church have ordained that no man shall be so hardy as to speak of God, for God almighty forbids not, sir, that we shall speak of Him. And also the Gospel makes mention that, when the woman had heard our Lord preach, she came before Him with a loud voice and said, 'Blessed be the womb that bore Thee and the teats that gave Thee suck'. Then our Lord said back to her, 'Truly, so are they blessed that hear the Word of God and keep it'. And therefore, sir, it seems to me that the Gospel gives me leave to speak of God.

The Archbishop's clerks at this point observed that 'she has a devil within her, for she speaks of the Gospel', and 'a great clerk' brought forth a book and 'laid Saint Paul for his part against her, that no woman should preach'. Her reply on that occasion was to say, 'I preach not, sir; I come to no pulpit. I use but communication and good words and that will I do while I live.' Eventually the Archbishop asked, 'Where shall I get a man who might lead this woman from me?', dismissed as unsuitable the young men who volunteered, picked a 'good sober man' of his own household and paid him five shillings to get her out of his region. 'She, kneeling down on her knees, asked his blessing. He, praying her to pray for him, blessed her and let her go.'

Much later in her *Book* Margery Kempe tells of Christ reminding her that he had once sent St Paul to her to strengthen and comfort her, so that she should speak boldly in Christ's name.[48] 'And St Paul said to you that you had suffered much tribulation because of his writing, and he promised you that because of this you should have as much grace for his love as you ever had shame or reproof for his love', which was one way of claiming for herself at the least what St Paul allowed to the women of Corinth. At any rate, we might think that Virginia Woolf might have approved of her, and she might have put her in the tradition of those whom she called the prophetesses,[49] even if, like Emily Brontë, of whom she certainly approved, she could not have been given authority in the Church conceded by ordination, not even to the extent permitted to the women deacons of the Church of England ordained in the spring of 1987. Virginia Woolf quotes Emily Brontë's 1846 poem, the one which begins

> No coward soul is mine
> No trembler in the world's storm-troubled sphere,
> I see Heaven's glories shine,
> And Faith shines equal arming me from fear.
>
> O God within my breast,
> Almighty, ever-present Deity!
> Life—that in me has rest,
> As I—undying Life—have power in Thee!

Virginia Woolf also examines in some detail one of the silliest documents on the ordination of women ever penned, even by English-speaking ecclesiastics, namely the report of the Archbishops' Commission of 1936, which expresses attitudes which still confuse thought about how to use the gifts of those women who wish to serve the gospel. The Commission's statement of opinion could be used to argue *for* rather than against the ordination of women, quite apart from ecclesiastical ignorance about the way in which women members of a congregation may regard their minister. The crucial paragraph is quoted by Monica Furlong:

> We maintain that the ministration of women will tend to produce a lowering of the spiritual tone of Christian worship, such as is not produced by the ministrations of men before congregations largely or exclusively female. It is a tribute to the quality of Christian womanhood that it is possible to make this statement; but it would appear to be a simple matter of fact that in the thoughts and desires of that sex the natural is more easily made subordinate to the supernatural, the carnal to the spiritual, than is the case with men; and that the ministrations of a male priesthood do not normally arouse that side of female nature which should be quiescent during the times of the adoration of Almighty God. We believe, on the other hand, that it would be impossible for the male members of the average congregation to be present at a service at which a woman ministered without becoming unduly conscious of her sex.[50]

The new women deacons may well prove to be a source of disturbance, but may like to take heart from the advice which Leslie Stephen (no mean patriarch himself) gave to his daughter, and which she repeated in 1940, exhorting workers, women, commoners and critics. Virginia Woolf repeated his advice by inviting her hearers to 'bear in mind a piece of advice that an eminent Victorian who was also an eminent pedestrian once gave to walkers: "Whenever you see a board up with 'Trespassers will be prosecuted', trespass at once."'[51] Having as it were developed the habit of trespassing, however, and having found their voices, the problem is and will be to identify what it is that women think that they as women will find to say about divine reality. Will it ever be possible to develop a thealogy? It is doctrines of God which must remain an important and essential focus of attention in any discussion of the relation between Christianity and feminism and it is to certain elements in these doctrines that I turn in my final chapter.

Notes

1   Elisabeth Moltmann-Wendel, *The Women around Jesus*, pp. 15–30.
2   Nancy Ore in Rosemary Radford Ruether, *Womanguides*, pp. 153–5.
3   Sharon H. Ringe, 'A Gentile Woman's Story' in Russell (ed.), *Feminist Interpretation of the Bible*, pp. 65–72.
4   See Mary Evans, *Woman in the Bible* (Paternoster Press 1983).
5   See Mary Hayter, *The New Eve in Christ* (SPCK 1987), pp. 119f.
6   Morna D. Hooker, 'Authority on her Head: An Examination of 1 Cor. 11.10' in *New Testament Studies*, 10 (1963–), pp. 410–16.
7   See also Clark, *Women in the Early Church*, on Chrysostom's commentary on 1 Tim. 2.11–15, pp. 156–60; Laporte, *The Role of Women in Early Christianity*, pp. 119–24.
8   Morley, 'The Faltering Words of Men', p. 64.
9   See for instance, Ann Phillips (ed.), *A Newnham Anthology* (Cambridge University Press 1979).
10   Virginia Woolf, *A Room of One's Own*, 1st pub. 1929 (Panther 1985).
11   Quentin Bell, *Virginia Woolf 2. Mrs Woolf 1912–1941* (Hogarth Press 1972), p. 144.
12   Woolf, *A Room of One's Own*, pp. 21–2.
13   ibid., p. 36.
14   Mary Daly, *Beyond God the Father*, 1st pub. 1973 (Women's Press 1985), pp. 195–8.
15   Woolf, *The Years*, 1st pub. 1937 (Granada 1982), pp. 275–6.
16   Woolf, *A Room of One's Own*, p. 43.
17   ibid., p. 49.
18   ibid., pp. 49–50.
19   Woolf, *Three Guineas* 1st pub. 1938 (Hogarth Press 1986).
20   ibid., p. 189.
21   ibid., p. 188.
22   Jane Marcus, 'Thinking Back through our Mothers' in Jane Marcus (ed.), *New Feminist Essays on Virginia Woolf* (Macmillan 1981), pp. 1–30.
23   ibid., p. 23.
24   ibid., p. 24.
25   ibid., p. 25.
26   Michèle Barrett (ed.), *Virginia Woolf: Women and Writing* (Women's Press 1979), p. 59.
27   Valerie Saiving, 'The Human Situation: A Feminine View' in Carol P. Christ and Judith Plaskow (eds.), *Womanspirit Rising* (New York, Harper & Row, 1979) pp. 25–42; Herbert Anderson, *The Family and Pastoral Care* (Philadelphia, Fortress Press, 1984).
28   Margaret Fell, *Women's speaking justified, proved and allowed of by the Scriptures, all such as speak by the spirit and power of the Lord Jesus. And how women were the first that preached the tidings of the resurrection of Jesus, and were sent by Christ's own command, before he ascended to the Father, John 20.17*, 1st pub. 1666. Republished Amherst, Mass., for the Mosher Book and Tract Committee, New England Yearly Meeting of Friends, 1980.

29   Retha M. Warnicke, *Women of the English Renaissance and Reformation* (Greenwood 1983), chapter on 'The Catholic Women of Elizabethan England'.

30   'Notebook' in *The Tablet* (26 January 1985). See also 'Mary Ward: Essays in Honour of the Fourth Centenary of her Birth' in *The Way Supplement*, 53 (1985); Margaret Mary Littlehales, IBVM, *Mary Ward: A Woman for All Seasons* (Catholic Truth Society 1982); IBVM (ed.), *The Heart and Mind of Mary Ward* (Clarke 1985); Mathilde Köhler, *Maria Ward: ein Frauenschicksal des 17. Jahrhunderts* (Munich, Kösel-Verlag, 1984).

31   Linda Woodbridge, *Women and the English Renaissance: Literature and the Nature of Womankind, 1540–1620* (Harvester 1984), pp. 38f.

32   ibid., p. 41

33   In Julia O'Faolain and Lauro Martines (eds.), *Not in God's Image* (New York, Harper & Row, 1973), pp. 183–4.

34   Woodbridge, *Women and the English Renaissance*, p. 43.

35   *The Book of Margery Kempe*, tr. B. A. Windeatt (Penguin 1985), with a most helpful bibliography (p. 331–2) to which I am greatly indebted.

36   J. T. Hogg, 'Mount Grace Charterhouse and Late Medieval English Spirituality' in *Analecta Cartusiana* (1980), pp. 1–43. On Margurite Porete, see Dronke, *Women Writers of the Middle Ages*, pp. 217f; Elizabeth Alvilda Petroff, *Medieval Women's Visionary Literature*, pp. 294f.

37   See Beryl Smalley on Dom David Knowles' *The English Mystical Tradition* in *The Oxford Magazine* (30 November 1961); and Dom Alberic Stacpoole, 'The Making of a Monastic Historian 2' in *The Ampleforth Journal*, 80:2 (1975), pp. 19–38.

38   Simon Tugwell, *Ways of Imperfection: An Exploration of Christian Spirituality* (Darton, Longman & Todd 1984).

39   ibid., p. 39.

40   *The Book of Margery Kempe*, pp. 42–4.

41   ibid., pp. 217–19.

42   Rosemary Woolf, *The English Religious Lyric in the Middle Ages* (Oxford University Press 1968), p. 146, quoting John Pecham, Franciscan Archbishop of Canterbury:

> Happy he who at that time could attend the incomparable mother entreating her to be allowed once a day to kiss her sweet child and fondle Him. How pleasant a bath I would have prepared for Him, and how willingly would I have carried the water on my shoulders; I would always have been at hand ministering to the Virgin Mother and I would have washed the tiny rags of the baby born so poor.

43   Windeatt's notes to *The Book of Margery Kempe*, p. 308.

44   Anthony Goodman, 'The Piety of John Brunham's daughter of Lynne' in Derek Baker (ed.), *Medieval Women* (Basil Blackwell 1978), pp. 347–58, esp. p. 355.

45   Claire Cross, '"Great Reasoners in Scripture": The Activities of Women Lollards 1380–1530' in Baker, op. cit., pp. 359–80.

46   See Joanna Ziegler, 'Women of the Middle Ages: Some Questions Regarding the Béguines and Devotional Art' in *Vox Benedictina*, 3:4 (1986),

pp. 338–57, on the emergence of the Pièta in the early fourteenth century; and see Edith Pargeter's *The Heaven Tree* trilogy, 1 (Macdonald 1986), pp. 335–7, on Madonna Benedetta's desire for the care, most of all when dead, of Harry Talvace's body, to which she is bound by Harry's enemy and her former lover, whom she defies. With Harry's body she is thrown into the river, rescued from it by the archer who co-operated with her to secure for Harry a quick death and save him from a traitor's death at the hands of Isambard's executioner. The archer thus enables her to become the one who saves Harry's young wife and newly born son—a secular 'Pièta' story?

47   Using William Provost's version of part of the text in Katharina M. Wilson (ed.), *Medieval Women Writers* (Athens, Georgia University Press, 1984), pp. 314–17.

48   *The Book of Margery Kempe*, pp. 199–200.

49   Woolf, *Three Guineas*, pp. 141–2.

50   In her introduction to Monica Furlong (ed.), *Feminine in the Church* (SPCK) 1984), p. 2.

51   Quoted in Lyndall Gordon, *Virginia Woolf: A Writer's Life* (Oxford University Press 1984), p. 261.

5

GOD AND GOD-ESS

Language about divine reality

In this part of my study I want to look at two topics affected by 'gender', which, as I said in my first chapter, I take to mean what any given society makes of the biological differences which make some of us women and some of us men. The concluding part of my discussion will concern itself with what we might call whimpers, bangs, and the question of whether we can call the deity 'mother'. My first part, however, is about what feminist theologians make of Mary the mother of Jesus, since it is sometimes thought that those who use the symbolism associated with 'Mary' are somehow spared from changing the range of their language about the deity. I write 'Mary' to indicate the weight of that symbolism, and Mary (without inverted commas), when I mean the name of the particular historical woman who was the mother of Jesus of Nazareth. Beginning with 'Mary' also enables me to pick up some of the concerns of my earlier chapters especially, beginning with a passage from Elizabeth Cady Stanton's *The Woman's Bible* first of all—a passage by one of her collaborators. This writer has muddled several doctrines together, but nevertheless manages to make a point about the way in which these doctrines have been and still are 'read' by women, no matter what is said to them about what the doctrines are *supposed* to mean, according to those who understand the terms of their definitions. Women continue to misread these doctrines, and in a sense this is inevitable, because they make connections between the doctrines and tacit messages as it were passed to them in ways of which they may be only half aware. Elizabeth Cady Stanton's collaborator seems to have written in some desperation from within the nineteenth-century context of hopelessly idealized maternalism:

> I think that the doctrine of the Virgin Birth as something higher, sweeter, nobler than ordinary motherhood, is a slur on all the natural motherhood of the world. I believe that millions of children have been as immaculately conceived, as purely born, as was the Nazarene. Why not? Out of this doctrine, and that which is akin to it, have

sprung all the monasteries and nunneries of the world, which have disgraced and distorted and demoralised manhood and womanhood for a thousand years. I place beside the false, monkish, unnatural claim of the Immaculate Conception my mother, who was as holy in her motherhood as was Mary herself.[1]

Leaving aside for the moment the problems raised by Christian asceticism at its worst rather than its best, I want to draw attention to the way in which doctrines about 'Mary', including that of the 'Immaculate Conception' are consistently assessed by women (even when *theoretical* understanding has been achieved) as suggesting the denigration of all other women who are mothers. This assessment has been learned from the Christian tradition itself. Even without expressly defined dogma, a *Kontakion* popular in the Orthodox tradition which was written most probably in Constantinople during the first half of the seventh century (recently translated for the ESBVM) hails 'Mary' for instance as 'thou who alone art blameless and fair among women';[2] and the 'Te Deum' sung at Anglican Matins includes as a reflection on the divine self-emptying, 'When thou tookest upon thee to deliver man thou didst not abhor the Virgin's womb.' Quite apart from the astonishing prurience displayed in devotion to 'Mary' on the part of some of her adherents,[3] not the least remarkable feature of Christian tradition is the extreme rarity of the sane comment made by the ninth-century Ratramnus, attempting to combat beliefs consequent upon the assumption that the womb was impure, when he insists, first, that no creature was created vile, and 'Hence also a woman's uterus is not indecent, but honourable.'[4] For sheer punitive nastiness, there is little to beat the comment made by Suarez in 1584, who wrote of that 'troublesome weariness with which all pregnant women are burdened, she alone did not experience who alone conceived without pleasure'.[5] Another gem from the writings of a seventeenth-century male saint observes that 'It is a subject of humiliation of all the mothers of the children of Adam to know that while they are with child, they carry within them an infant... who is the enemy of God, the object of his hatred and malediction and the shrine of the demon.'[6] This is at once a 'theological' response to the sheer difficulties of childbearing, from pregnancy, through birth to lactation and weaning, the risks to the mother, and to the high

79

mortality rate among children until comparatively recent times, as well as being a preface to the assertion of the need for 'rebirth' by baptism, male-administered. What it may also express to women is the theology of 'God punished women more', which in the nineteenth and early twentieth century hindered the use of anaesthetic and analgesic drugs in childbirth, even when these had become comparatively safe and available. [7]

Let us go on to Mary Daly's very controversial assessment of the 1854 treatment of the dogma of the 'Immaculate Conception', one of two dogmas which have not only proved troublesome to women, but also to the relationship between the Roman Catholic Church and the Orthodox Churches, as well as to Protestant Churches. Mary Daly[8] acknowledges that 'Mary' has been for many women their only symbol of hope, not least when they have been on 'spiritual starvation rations'. Yet for Mary Daly, 'Mary' is 'killed' by the dogmas about her, killed, though apparently alive, like a dolled-up Christmas tree. She points out that the 1854 definition coincides with the first wave of feminism. Here is a woman preserved from original sin by the grace of her son, not only in advance of *his* birth but of *her own*. What she is purified from is her own autonomous being; her psyche is already dismembered; and the story of the Annunciation, affirming her need of male acceptance—'according to thy will'—makes her doubly a victim. She then functions only as a token woman of hope, since she stands over against the incompetence and array of weaknesses ascribed to women in general. So for Mary Daly the impossible ideal of Virgin/Mother has ultimately a punitive function, since no actual woman can live up to it, throwing all women back into the status of Eve and essentially reinforcing the universality of women's low-caste status. [9]

This is perhaps a convenient point to couple with her opinions of the 1854 dogma Mary Daly's treatment of the 1950 dogma of the Assumption, which of course *can* mean, and not before time, saying 'no' to the association of women peculiarly with sin and the flesh and with matter—all alike to be repudiated by those unable to distinguish detestation of sin from disgust with themselves and their own bodies. For Mary Daly, the 1950 dogma again coincided with the post-World War II backlash *against* female independence. When the war was over, for a time,

so were some female gains. This dogma then annihilates
woman's earthly presence, and rehabilitates her as defeated,
eliminated from public life, 'saved', once again, by the male.[10]
Even making allowances for Mary Daly's acerbity, this takes us
into another very difficult area, the one indicated by the
question, 'Can a male Christ save women?' Medieval women
theologians coped with this question via the analogy of 'male is
to female as form is to matter' by identifying with Christ in his
physicality. For some, 'Mary' was the *tunica humanitatis*, the clothing
of humanity that God put on in the Incarnation. So Caroline
Walker Bynum writes of *some* thirteenth-century women that
they had an intense conviction of their ability to imitate Christ
without role or gender inversion. 'To soar towards Christ as
lover and bride, to sink into the stench and torment of the
crucifixion, to eat God, was for the woman only to give religious
significance to what she already was.'[11] If matter was redeemed,
women were especially saved by the Incarnation.

The problem now is that the analogy of 'male is to female as
form is to matter', is no longer defensible, any more than is the
thesis that 'the first and principal cause of offspring is always in
the father'. Marina Warner quotes the passage in Aeschylus'
Oresteia, where Orestes at his trial cries out in protest, 'And dost
thou call *me* a blood relation of my mother?' Apollo arbitrates
with the judgement that 'The so-called offspring is not produced
by the mother ... She is not more than the nurse as it were, of the
newly conceived foetus. It is the male who is the author of its
being.'[12] This has been untenable without considerable qualifi-
cation since the development of embryology from the early
nineteenth century onwards, but it still influences doctrines
about the ministry as it does doctrines about 'Mary'. So in the
Bishop of London's November 1985 newsletter he did his best to
elaborate the view that 'in the whole of human instinct and
understanding it is the masculine which is associated with giving
and the feminine with receiving', a remark liable to produce
much hilarity in women who have become aware of and
articulate about their role in securing the wellbeing of men,
without any expectation that the converse will obtain. In Marian
doctrines we can still see the influence of this theory, which has
to do with what a culture thinks reproduction is all about, that is,
'the relationship between procreative beliefs and the wider

81

context (world view, cosmology, culture) in which they are found'.[13] Paternity, in Carol Delaney's analysis, has meant 'the primary, essential and creative role' in reproduction, and the meaning of maternity is epitomized by 'Mary'. Carol Delaney takes the root meanings of 'Virgin Birth' (and we may add the dogmas already mentioned) to be versions of folk-theories about procreation, the essential implication of which is that a child originates from only *one* source; thus they are entirely consistent with theological monotheism. Carol Delaney's fieldwork in a Turkish Muslim village enabled her to identify an appropriate theory of procreation, which is that 'The male is said to plant the seed and the woman is said to be like a field', so the woman's role is secondary, supportive and nurturant. So she identifies the analogy 'Woman is to Man as the created, natural world is to God,' and we can connect this with metaphors from the *Kontakion* of the seventh century mentioned earlier and with a poem closely associated with it from the sixth century. First, *Kontakion* Two: 'Then the power of the Most High overshadowed her that knew not wedlock, so that she might conceive: and he made her fruitful womb as a fertile field for all who long to reap the harvest of salvation, singing: Alleluia!'[14] Second, amongst the riot of metaphors in the poem, the so-called 'Standing hymn', we find Mary urged by the unborn John in Elizabeth's womb to rejoice as the 'vine with unwithering shoot', 'farm with untainted fruit', 'arable yielding a bountiful stack of pity', 'furbishing a lush pasturage'.[15] Carol Delaney is surely correct to point out that the knowledge that women are 'co-engenderers, co-creators, providing half the "seed" so to speak, half the genetic constitution of the child in addition to pregnancy, birth and suckling, has not yet been encompassed symbolically'. Paternity is indeed a cultural construction of a powerful kind, and one cannot simply claim that the meaning of 'Mary's' virginity is that 'the role played by the human race in the Incarnation is simply that of accepting God's gift as a gift and as a grace, and nothing more',[16] correct though that is so far as it goes. How that claim is to be received by women given its association with these other elements in the tradition which I have mentioned remains something of a problem.

My concern at this point however is with what Elizabeth Cady Stanton's collaborator called 'the false, monkish element in

Christianity', and how it may connect with asceticism at its worst as well as with the 'Aristotelian' view of paternity discussed above. For those to whom Christianity offered a new kind of aspiration, the virgin 'Mary' was a possible symbol of their discipleship which took overriding priority in their lives. As I noted in chapter 2, to be sexually virginal was to be freed from a measure of male domination; so sexual asceticism was not therefore necessarily imposed on women as a kind of constraint. Sarah Maitland's brilliant novel, *Daughter of Jerusalem* (1978), catches this element in virginity beautifully in her initial reflection on 'Mary', small, dark, devout, probably illiterate, unconventional, of unassailable self-assurance:

> Of course her assent is a sexual act, she tried to explain, pushing her hair back under her scarf, and grinding her bare toes into the coarse sand, because it was complete, it was made with the whole of her being. It was an assent to the totality of herself, to a womanhood so vital and empowered that it could break free of biology and submission, any dependence on or need for a masculine sexuality— that furrow in which the crop of women's sex has been held to be rooted.'[17]

However, as we also saw, it is easy to forget that virginity could signal a vocation if it was praised by undoubted woman-haters, even making the most generous allowances in the interpretation of the rhetoric of misogyny. When males are taken to be the normative and representative and essentially life-giving expression of the human species, with females as defective, imperfect and 'merely' nurturant human beings, then virginity can change its significance, and come to mean an attempt to approximate to an ideal that one can never reach, and this is as much the case when the ideal is 'Mary' as when the ideal is male. If we could retrieve from the tradition the association of 'virgin' with autonomy, and *without* the abasement of a woman's visual image,[18] and associate autonomy with the affirmation and not the negation of what women discover themselves to be, then we might be able to reconnect 'Mary' to the needs of twentieth-century women, as, for instance, Rosemary Radford Ruether attempts to do.[19]

Ruether, like Mary Daly, wants female presence acknowledged without fear of real women, but she also wants the co-ordination of nature and grace recovered for those whose ecclesiastical traditions have lost it—again (against Daly) arguably expressed in 'Mary's' rapturous assent; as well as the genuine reciprocity of women and men together in the Churches. Furthermore, she ties the *Magnificat* in to the revolutionary spirit of liberation theology, with women above all representing the 'nobodies' made to be persons as a result of the self-emptying of divine power in Jesus. To that I think I would want to add two other points.

Marina Warner[20] spots in 'Mary' something else that matters, explained oddly enough in the *Times* of 7 February 1987 by Rabbi Ephraim Gastwirth, though he apparently disapproves of what he describes, preferring rather 'the love and fear of a stern father'. Mother, he tells us, has a love which is eternal and her broad arms encompass all her children without distinction. 'Indeed, her love is often stronger for the weak and wayward child, seeking to ensure his survival and to keep him within the family group. The mother's love is unconditional.' There is a sense in which 'Mary' is as splendidly unconventional as Jesus was, since her loyalty to her own explodes the bounds of strict justice, as Marina Warner makes clear. 'Through her the whole gay crew of wanton, loving, weak humanity finds its way to paradise.' She quotes the devils who say 'Heaven's the place for all the riff-raff/We've got the wheat and God the chaff.'[21] This association of 'Mary' with unconditional and unconventional love and with self-determination, relates her back to some less hallowed women, taking a clue from the genealogy of the first Gospel: women such as Ruth, Tamar, Rahab and Bathsheba. We need to connect 'Mary' to the other women of the apostolic tradition, including the woman who wiped Jesus' feet with her hair, and the others whom I have mentioned, such as the Syro-Phoenician, Martha, the Samaritan woman of John 4, Mary of Magdala, Phoebe the deacon and many more.

Thus to my second point, culled from Elizabeth Moltmann-Wendel's assessment of the 'Mary' tradition.[22] She wants both more honesty about the biblical origins of the 'Mary' tradition, and makes us see Mary as a 'living critical, angry unadapted mother', just as human and as difficult as some of the other people around Jesus, men as well as women. She emphasizes that Mary needs to take her place, perhaps a pre-eminent place, but only one place, amongst all these other 'sisters'.[23] For perhaps one of the greatest defects of the 'Mary' tradition in the past has been its monolithic character, the attempt to load into one symbol almost everything women can represent in human life. Feminist theologians who follow her lead will not want Mary confined by ecclesiastical definition however subtle: they want to be able to relate her to other women and the multiplicity of vocations and possibilities of their lives now and in the future. Even those who want what she means to them to be expressed in those dogmas, or whose convictions are expressed in the poetry of their liturgies, are unable to avoid the points made by Eric Doyle in his paper on 'God and the feminine'.

> That a woman stood at the most crucial point in salvation history, that her *fiat* belongs to official, public, saving history in the economy of God, that she is depicted by the most venerable and ancient Christian writers as Archetype of the Church—all this provides weighty grounds for inquiring into the question of whether Mary, as a woman who is a mother, reveals an aspect of God's life and nature; that is to say, whether womanhood and motherhood have their source in God.[24]

For him, Mary's significance is that 'she makes us look beyond herself for the source of what she is by nature and grace'. This is the point, then, at which I turn to consider some of the problems connected with theology and feminine gender, the topic which lies at the heart of the debate about Christianity and feminism.

In my first chapter I said that I took gender to mean what any given society makes of the biological differences which make some of us women and some of us men. I also commented that, so far as I can see, the empirical study of gender is often controversial within its own field, and that gender issues can polarize social scientists almost faster than any other issue. I rely here on the work of Richard Kahoe in a recent paper in *Religious Studies Review*[25] on the social science of gender differences as an ideological battleground. He says that the majority *opinion* holds that: (1) save for essential reproductive functions, basic differences between men and women are trivial; (2) those differences are almost all due to socio-cultural influences, which (3) men control to maintain power over women. But *research* indicates that: (1) substantial differences distinguish the human genders; (2) many of these are based on biology; (3) fundamental power belongs to women as much as to men. So far, not so good.

The problem is that conclusions about how to construe what

purports to be evidence can be biased by ideologies, and ardent feminists can be so biased by 'male' ideology that women press for identity with men, and this both in religious traditions and outside them. Yet, despite the problems, gender has become an important category of analysis in examining religious traditions, and especially how religious traditions not only reflect particular social assumptions about gender, but in their turn may shape and re-shape these assumptions. I am not going to run through some of the empirical data about gender differences, but I would like to quote one important feature of Kahoe's remarks, those on physical health, which I think are peculiarly relevant to the ways in which women have seen it to be their responsibility to secure the wellbeing of men. Kahoe points out:

> Boys initially show more physical problems than girls. For every 100 females conceived, 120—140 males are conceived, but by the end of normal pregnancy, spontaneous abortions leave but 106 males to 100 females. Although boy babies average 5 per cent heavier, they are four to six weeks behind girls in physical maturity. More males are stillborn or born blind. 70 per cent of all other birth defects occur more commonly in boys than in girls. In the first few months, 30 per cent more males than females die, and they suffer more from almost all childhood diseases. By puberty the male female ratio is about equal.[26]

Boys have been, or are, more difficult to rear, but having been reared, as we interpret the process, mother has to be denied for a boy to maintain and develop his sense of self, so that he can become independent, strong and autonomous. I will come back later to a different kind of empirical evidence (different, that is, from Kahoe's) to suggest how this connects with the problem of calling God mother. For the moment, I simply want to remind you of another point that I made earlier, which is that it is difficult consistently to remind ourselves that theology is itself a gender-related term for our naming and talking about divine reality, assuming that there is a divine reality about which we can intelligibly talk. It is surprisingly difficult to be sensitive to this, that God is *not* anthropomorphically merely feminine, but not anthropomorphically merely masculine either. Having said that, the complaint all too obviously is that divine reality *has* been conceived of in predominantly masculine terms in Christianity, and, furthermore, this caveat about the importance of the *negative* in our language concerning that reality has been too readily forgotten.

If anyone is unclear about all this, or about how offensive it can seem to women, perhaps I can give one example, from Scott Holland's own essay on faith in *Lux Mundi* (1889). You may recall that in my first chapter I said that Scott Holland was undoubtedly sensitive to the problems women faced in his lifetime, was well aware of the need 'to secure for women an entirely new value and significance', and thought that it was a matter of Christian responsibility to secure it, with women themselves bringing their convictions and experiences to bear on the discussion of their claims and wrongs. In *Lux Mundi* he wrote of 'thirsts', which faith had not prepared itself to satisfy; yet there is in Scott Holland's own writing only too much evidence of the habits of thought and expression which are now seen to be so irritating to women. To understand faith, he tells us, we have to keep close to the conception of sonship. As a result perhaps of his meditation on St John's gospel, he writes that 'Faith is the attitude, the temper, of a son towards a father. That is a relationship we can all understand for ourselves', that is, a relationship which is such that love is one with reverence and duty fulfils itself in joy. Such a sonship is one which renders to the son 'every mood and gesture of the father.'

> His very blood moves in rhythm to the father's motives. His soul hangs, for guidance, on the father's eyes: to him, each motive of the father justifies itself as a satisfying inspiration. The father's will is felt deliciously encompassing him about; enclosed within it, his own will works, glad and free in its fortifying obedience. Such a relationship as this needs no justifying sanction beyond itself: it is its own sanction, its own authority, its own justification. 'He is my father': that is a sufficient reason for all this sympathetic response to another's desire. 'I am his son': that is the final premiss in which all argument comes to a close.[27]

Later he adds that

> Our manhood lies in this essential sonship: and if so, then to be without faith, without the conscious realisation of the sonship, is to be without the fulness of a man's proper nature. It is to be inhuman: to be curtailed of the natural development: to be maimed and thwarted. It means that the vital outcome of the inner verity has been arrested; that the sensitive perceptions have been blunted and stunted . . . '[28]

Of these passages it could of course be said that one might want to discuss the character of the father-son relationship, about which we seem to know remarkably little as compared with the mother-son relationship, and that relationship as described in the first passage quoted is curious, to say the least, coming from a member of a family in which according to one of Scott Holland's brothers, his father lived reserved, like a born bachelor, and in which the family's devotion was poured out on to their mother. Scott Holland himself seems to have found his intellectual and emotional match in one of his unmarried aunts.[29] For all his undoubted sympathies with women in his society (and his delight in the company of even the newest baby), he betrays absolutely no perception at all that those passages cannot, except by some complicated process of erasure, transcription and transposition, be read as an exercise in inclusive language, in which women can read what faith might mean for them. Nor, with regard to the second passage, are women prepared to accept that they are inhuman, maimed, thwarted, blunted or stunted because they cannot perceive what 'sonship' means as the pattern of faith.

Scott Holland might have been allowed to get away with some of what he is trying to say if he had consistently talked of a child's, rather than of a son's, relationship to its father, and included the mother's relationship to the child too, except that elsewhere in the essay he talks about the early beginnings of faith as 'a power still in the womb—still unborn into its true sphere—still enveloped in dark wrapping which encumber and impede'.[30] This might be an acceptable metaphor, but again, he goes on to discuss the need to talk not in the babble of pretty baby language but in a language level with its work, and 'its work is complicated, hard and disciplined'.[31] Faith, he tells us, is the inspiration of innate sonship, breeding confidence, secure of itself, undaunted, unfatigued. Further, that sonship abides 'in us all', though it is 'cumbered and clouded' by our sin. It abides in us, 'fed by the succours of a Father who can never forget or forsake, and Who is working hitherto to recover and redeem.'[32] It sounds as though one needs not only to be born again, but to be born male, and then to learn the father's language, to tackle the world's work. One might say that the women of this man's household have done their work well, having nurtured a man still dependent upon them, but with the dependence camouflaged, so that he sees himself as strong and autonomous in his identification with his father, and in his heavenly father's identification of him with Christ.

Another illustration of this which we might cite is to be found in one of Hopkins' poems:

> I say more: the just man justices;
> Keeps grace: that keeps all his goings graces;
> Acts in God's eye what in God's eye he is—
> Christ—for Christ plays in ten thousand places,
> Lovely in limbs, and lovely in eyes not his
> To the Father through the features of men's faces.[33]

Women have become too uncomfortable with this way of construing the kind of relationship they may have with divine reality, since they find that it is consistently employed to exclude their experience. Thus they may want to dispense with it, even if it distresses them to do so in the process of having to find a sense of self-worth proper to them.

Emily Dickinson in 1882 wrote

> Those—dying then,
> Knew where they went—
> They went to God's right hand—
> That Hand is amputated now
> And God cannot be found—[34]

Even more telling in the present context is Sylvia Plath's *Three Women*, a poem for three voices written in 1962 and set in a maternity ward and round about it.

> It is these men I mind;
> They are so jealous of anything that is not flat!
> They are jealous gods
> That would have the whole world flat because they
>   are.
> I see the Father conversing with the Son.
> Such flatness cannot but be holy.
> 'Let us make a heaven', they say.
> 'Let us flatten and launder the grossness from
>   these souls.'[35]

Karen Blixen said of the Holy Trinity that it was 'the most deadly dull of male companies'.[36]

Denied a language which seems appropriate to them, and which arises out of and gives expression to their perceptions of reality and of divine reality, some women want to overturn the Christian tradition *by means of* the tradition, and thus reshape it in possibly unforeseeable ways. They have scavenged for what there is to be found there, to reclaim it from assimilation to masculine understanding. Scott Holland wrote of being fed by the succour of a Father who can never forget or forsake, which reminds us to look at some of the Old Testament feminine-related imagery for the divine. The particular passage to which Scott Holland was alluding is refreshingly free of naive idealism about maternity. For to ask, 'Can a woman forget her sucking child, that she should have no compassion on the son of her womb?' is to answer that she may, in order to point up by contrast the divine and maternal promise, 'Yet I will not forget you. Behold I have graven you upon the palms of my hands' (Isa. 49.15).

Feminine-related imagery for God in the Old Testament includes that of a woman in labour (Isa. 42.14); a comforting mother (Isa. 66.12–13). And so Job addressed God:

> Didst thou not pour me out like milk
> and curdle me like cheese?
> Thou didst clothe me with skin and flesh,
> and knit me together with bones and sinews.
> Thou has granted me life and steadfast love
> and thy care has preserved my spirit (10.10–12).

All of this makes his agony of apparent abandonment worse, the same point implicit in Psalm 22, which begins, 'My God, my God, why hast thou forsaken me?' yet is addressed to the God 'who took me from the womb':

> thou didst keep me safe upon my mother's breasts.
> Upon thee was I cast from my birth,
> and since my mother bore me thou hast been my
> God (22.9–10).

God as mother or midwife is perhaps best indicated by Isaiah 46.4: 'I have made and I will bear; I will carry and will save.'[37] Phyllis Trible's *God and the Rhetoric of Sexuality*[38] has made the most of what there is to be found, but it still has to be acknowledged that in the Old Testament the deity is not called 'Mother' or addressed as 'Mother' directly, nor does the demonstration that 'to show mercy' is connected with the root word for 'womb' tell us much about the association of women's 'gut-reactions' with the activity of showing mercy on the part of those who did, let alone with their hearts and minds when they described the deity as merciful.[39]

Other women theologians, Joan Chamberlain Engelsman,[40] for instance, have worked out the way in which divine reality and activity is conveyed by some elements of the 'Wisdom' tradition, in which 'wisdom', a feminine noun, is sometimes associated with 'spirit', also feminine in Hebrew, and with 'Torah', also feminine. Her thesis is that 'wisdom' gets displaced in the Christian tradition by 'Logos', masculine, when doctrines of Christ were worked out, and thus *direct* access to the feminine divine is, so to speak, blocked out. Some of 'wisdom's' quasi-divine attributes get shifted on to the Church (and one practical thing about which we could all agree is to refuse to refer to the Church as a 'she', with or without quasi-divine attributes) and others, in time, on to Mary the mother of Jesus, who has a disturbing habit of emerging in her own right with all the attributes associated with goddesses, clearly one of the features of Christianity which makes it acceptable as a religion in many different cultures.

In the early patristic tradition it seems not to have been entirely forgotten that the 'spirit' of God could be appropriately indicated by a 'she', and thus as 'Mother', and Elizabeth Moltmann-Wendel's book, *A Land Flowing with Milk and Honey* (1986) documents and illustrates the ways in which this element of theology surfaced from time to time in some places and circumstances, in one case at least under the influence of Jewish mysticism. A cynic might, of course, comment that it is the lingering sense of the 'spirit' as 'she' which may have had so lamentable an effect on trinitarian doctrines, with the 'spirit' barely given 'substance' since 'she' seems to exist only in the relation between the Father and the Son.

Far more powerful, however, has been the 'Jesus as mother' element in the tradition, and I will try to indicate some of its features. My fundamental problem with it is that it seems to be the tradition of the all-sufficient male all over again, androgynously all-competent, embodying female divine wisdom. So Clement of Alexandria:

Milk of the bride
Given of heaven,
Pressed from sweet breasts—

91

> Gifts of thy Wisdom—
> These thy little ones
> Draw for their nourishment;
> With infancy lips
> Filling their soul
> With spiritual savor
> From breasts of the Word.[41]

One can pick up developments of androgynous all-competence all over the place, and not least when Christ's pain on the cross is interpreted as the pain of labour, as in the fourteenth-century Birgitta of Sweden, for instance:

> By my suffering I gave birth to humanity as a Mother, and I brought them forth from the darkness of death to eternal day. By carrying them in my womb with great effort, I fulfilled all the prophecies. I nourished them with my milk, feeding them with my words and the laws of life.[42]

One more example we might take is from the twelfth century Aelred of Rievaulx:

> Then one of the soldiers opened his side with a lance and there came forth blood and water. Hasten, linger not, eat the honeycomb with your honey, drink your wine with your milk. The blood is changed into wine to gladden you, the water into milk to nourish you. From the rock streams have flowed for you, wounds have been made in his limbs, holes in the walls of his body, in which, like a dove, you may hide while you kiss them one by one. Your lips, stained with blood, will become like a scarlet ribbon and your word sweet.[43]

Caroline Bynum's book, *Jesus as Mother* (1982), includes a chapter on the twelfth-century male Cistercian communities and their use of maternal imagery for God. It complemented their use of maternal imagery for the duties of prelates and abbots, as those who in authority must nurture and be accessible to members of the community, so that all would achieve the goal of union with and intimate dependence upon God. Maternal imagery applied to God or Christ had at least one advantage: it could displace the imagery drawn from the Song of Songs, which required the male to describe himself as a female in response to the male deity. Since monastic life made much of inverting the values of the world—dancing on one's hands like an acrobat—the use of maternal imagery for God or themselves tells us nothing about whether they valued the women in the world beyond the confines of the cloister. There is plenty of evidence in the same period of male resistance to women wanting to join the new or reformed religious orders,[44] as well as of the feminine as symbols of physical and spiritual weakness, flesh, sinfulness, the inability to bear burdens or to resist temptations; the latter was one of the principal reasons why they were not to be allowed to exercise authority, least of all in preaching.

Nor can we make much of St Anselm's eleventh-century prayer to St Paul, in which both Paul and Christ are addressed as mothers. The prayer is attractive in parts because it reworks Matthew 23.37, Jesus' lament over Jerusalem. 'How often would I have gathered your children together as a hen gathers her brood under her wings, and you would not', itself a rephrasing of Isaiah 31.5: 'Like birds hovering, so the Lord of hosts will protect Jerusalem; he will protect and deliver it, he will spare and rescue it.' Anselm's prayer includes this passage:

And you, my soul, dead in yourself,
run under the wings of Jesus your mother
    and lament your griefs under his feathers.
Ask that your wounds may be healed,
    and that, comforted, you may live again.

Christ, my mother,
you gather your chickens under your wings;
this dead chicken of yours puts himself under
    those wings,
For by your gentleness the badly frightened
    are comforted,
by your sweet smell the despairing are revived,
your warmth gives life from the dead,
your touch justifies sinners.
Mother, know again your dead son,
both by the sign of your cross and the voice of
    his confession.
Warm your chicken, give life to your dead man,
    justify your sinner.[45]

Without some of the other associations of the 'Jesus as mother' tradition, this extended metaphor could seem to be very appealing, but Anselm has his metaphor under strict control and does not allow it to permeate other areas of his theology, brilliant and original though so much of it is. In his *Meditation on the Rationale of Faith* or *Monologion*, for example, he asks why he must use the

93

masculine language of Father, Son and Spirit (Latin: *spiritus*, masculine) for the 'persons' of the Trinity. Leaving 'Father' out of it as presumably non-negotiable, he asks himself why it is not reasonable to refer to the second and third 'persons' of the Trinity as mother and daughter, since both are truth and wisdom, *veritas et sapientia* (both feminine). He thinks it is more consistent to use the language of 'Son' for the second 'person', that is, the sonship of male doctrinal identity, and also called the third 'person' 'Father', because he maintains as a good Aristotelian, 'the first and principal cause of offspring is always in the father',[46] an axiom to which I have already given attention in discussing 'Mary'.

More constructive are Dame Julian of Norwich's fourteenth-century *Showings* (also from the Benedictine ethos), since Julian used the 'Jesus as mother' element in the tradition to help her rework her *trinitarian* theology in a way which did not seem to be possible for Anselm, though such a reworking may not have been her primary object in writing. She had desired three graces by the gift of God, the first of which was to have recollection of Christ's passion: 'I thought that I wished that I had been at that time with Mary Magdalen and with the others who were Christ's lovers, so that I might have seen with my own eyes our Lord's passion which he suffered for me, so that I might have suffered with him as others did who loved him.'[47] So she gives her readers a vision of Christ 'hanging up in the air as people hang up a cloth to dry', at the very least a moving and unusual meditation on the words 'I thirst' from the cross.[48] Because of these recollections, she is confident that 'every kind of thing will be well' and that 'everything has being through the love of God'. So, to give one very brief example, for her, the second 'person' of the Trinity 'is our Mother in nature in our substantial creation, in whom we are founded and rooted, and he is our Mother of mercy in taking our sensuality. And so our Mother is working on us in various ways, in whom our parts are kept undivided; for in our Mother Christ, we profit and increase... '[49]

Kari Elisabeth Børresen stresses that Julian's theology is a unique achievement, because in it the mother metaphor is central and not confined to Christ's human nature but integrated into a description of the trinitarian deity, notwithstanding her awareness that all human discourse about the deity is on the level of a child's ABC. So, as this commentator notes, 'her use of both female and male metaphors represents human fullness, and is therefore a better instrument for describing divine wholeness than the traditional andromorphic God-language'.[50] Yet it is also worth re-emphasizing Caroline Walker Bynum's observation that the theme of the motherhood of God is not necessarily a 'feminine insight,'[51] and from her studies of women's spirituality it is not clear that feminine imagery is necessarily particularly attractive to them, though it may be on occasion, as we can find in the writing of Thérèse of Lisieux, consoling a disheartened novice:

> You remind me of a tiny child who is beginning to try to stand up; but it simply cannot manage to do so. More than anything else it wants to get up the stairs to its mother, and so lifts its little foot to climb the first step. Vain effort! Each time it falls back. Look now, you be this tiny child, and go on lifting your little foot... the good God only asks you for good intentions. He looks down lovingly upon you from the head of the stairs, and soon He will be disarmed by your vain efforts, and will come down Himself to take you up in his arms.

According to Hans Urs von Balthasar, she discovered the key to the formulation of her own teaching in Isaiah 66.12-13: 'You shall be carried at the breasts, and upon the knees they shall caress you. As one whom the mother caresseth, so will I comfort you.' And so she wrote:

> O You who know how to mould the hearts of mothers... Your heart is more than motherly to me. At every moment You watch over me and protect me; when I call to You, You never hesitate. And if at times You seem to be hiding, You are still the one who comes and helps me to find you.[52]

A more recent example of the attempt to realize the meaning of faith through the mother in the context of family relationships is Margaret Hebblethwaite's *Motherhood and God*,[53] though it may be rather hard on the actual family of someone who wants to rework spirituality and theology in this kind of way!

Outside the monastic tradition, another clearly identifiable context in which the language for the motherhood of God appeared was in the movement associated with Joanna Southcott, who in the late eighteenth century had an experience which led her to suppose that she was the 'woman clothed with the sun' of the book of Revelation;[54] but it is mainly to be connected with the

Shaking Quakers, those who had broken away from the Society of Friends in 1747 to await the second coming of Christ. They were known as Shakers because their sense of Christ's presence was expressed in song, bodily gesture, ecstatic spontaneous dancing and in trembling. Ann Lee as a Quaker was imprisoned in a Manchester gaol for sabbath breaking, and when she prayed for strength, she was overwhelmed with a sense of Christ's presence.[55] The communities that she and others founded in North America scandalized those who did not belong to them, because they were communities of men and women living celibate lives together: for outrage at 'papist' practice, combined with an equality between women and men, seemed to strike at the roots of the social order of the day. The Shaker communities were pacifist, and this too was beyond the level of tolerance of non-Shakers at the time of the American war of Independence. Radical gospel values lived out in these communities and the 'counsel of peace'[56] between the women and men in them, enabled them to explore feminine as well as masculine metaphors for the divine being without the androgynous muddle of the medieval tradition, but as with those living in monastic communities, celibacy was the price for doing so. It was probably this Shaker tradition in its nineteenth-century manifestation of *lived* peaceableness and reconciliation between women and men which lies behind Elizabeth Cady Stanton's appropriation of a Zulu prayer which she had picked up from her reading of Colenso, a prayer which concluded, 'Under Thy hand I pass the day! under Thy hand I pass the night! Thou art my Mother, Thou my Father'.[57]

Suppose, however, being neither Benedictine, Cistercian, nor celibate Shakers, we were to try to shift a marginal element in the Christian tradition into the mainstream in spirituality *and* in doctrine, what effects might it have? What could we expect it to do for us? Those who want to revive and elaborate this language should beware of claiming too much for it. Take, for instance, Flew's notorious remarks, when discussing the meaning of religious language: 'Someone tells us that God loves us as a father loves his children. We are reassured. But then we see a child dying of inoperable cancer of the throat. His earthly father is driven frantic in his efforts to help, but his Heavenly Father reveals no obvious sign of concern.'[58] Substitute 'mother' all through, and the child will still die of inoperable cancer of the throat, just as one singer of Psalm 22 died on the cross. But the language might have a more limited task, assuming that over a period of time (not too generous), the Churches might get themselves sorted out so far as lectionaries, liturgies and ministry are concerned, which might help to clarify what, if anything, they wanted to remember and affirm about women, and how, if at all, the Churches see women as contributing to our understanding of our shared human existence. I have very little confidence that this programme is likely to be performed, looking at the likely cast-list, but let us suppose that it was well on the way to full dress-rehearsal stage, lights, music and so on. What then might the language of God as mother do for us?

I said towards the beginning of this chapter that I would refer to some empirical evidence of a particular kind, which I should like to employ to try to indicate an answer to this question. The evidence is to be found in the work of Luise Eichenbaum and Susie Orbach, notably in their book *What do Women Want?*[59] This argues that a male's needs are addressed without his having to confront them and spell them out. He expects them to be met and they are, so that he has the confidence to launch himself into being strong, independent and autonomous. Females, however, grow up realizing that no one regards it as their prime responsibility to take care of them emotionally. They do not have the consistent experience of this having been done for them, and they go through life protecting themselves from showing this. So everyone works with a lot of camouflage. *He* goes on being dependent on women who are apparently dependent, weak and helpless; *she* has an unending well of neediness too, but it is not expressed and never met, and girls do not receive enough nurture from their mothers to separate successfully from them.

It is alleged that women's support for one another is meant to repair some of the damage, but in the long term only changes in patterns of child-rearing with *both* parents involved will over a period of generations enable women to develop a complete and secure sense of self. Both sexes could come to accept that it is natural for us to have dependency needs; both could accept that those needs require to be met so that both can become responsibly autonomous *in relation to one another*, without wearing all the camouflage. 'Fatherhood' in God and Church clearly continues to provide some women with the nurture that they need, but it is clearly failing many. Would 'Motherhood' in God help? Only, it seems to me, if Churches using the language in prayer, liturgy and doctrine were to constitute themselves as the kinds of communities where there were genuine attempts to try to repair the damage to women, as women's groups are alleged to do. So women might find either in women's groups or preferably and eventually in mixed-sex groups within the Churches something of that co-inherence they need to share outside the Church, or as my former tutor put it (though I hasten to stress not in this connection) hints of grace, bearing with corruption, rescuing and regenerating them.[60]

Yet even suppose that Churches were to become such communities of nurture for adults of both sexes, is there not still a major problem for post-Freudian and post-Feuerbachian twentieth-century people about using parental language for God at all? There is I think a major theological problem in using parental language for God, when we already know that it can be such a barrier to religious belief, depending on how the whole package of that belief is expressed and lived. Jacques Pohier's *God in Fragments* again seems to me to be remarkably perceptive when he says, for instance:

> It took me a long time to note the hatred of God engendered and disguised by the representations of him through the figures of Father and Son. It took me more effort, and involved more setbacks and evasions, to accept that the representation of God as the radical origin and the ultimate and unique goal of our existence engendered and disguised a hatred towards him for which only hatred of the mother could provide a relatively adequate image.[61]

A concluding comment: it is obvious that I have not attempted a reconstruction of what we might say about divine reality, though I think I can now see what such a reconstruction is going to involve. For me, co-inherence and mutuality between women and men must be expressed both in theology and in the institutions, symbols and roles, of which that theology is an expression and to which it may give direction. Early Christianity or past Christianity of any period is not less but no more than what Elisabeth Schüssler Fiorenza has called a prototype, 'critically open to the possibility of its own transformation'.[62] Also, I share her view that we must reclaim women's bodies and lives as 'the image and body of Christ',[63] in such a way as to speak of divine reality in a manner that does better justice to what women believe and to the ways in which they can live. We may need Elisabeth Schüssler Fiorenza's talk of Jesus' 'Sophia-God'[64] and certainly we must take seriously Kari Elisabeth Børresen's insistence that we need both female and male metaphors to indicate divine wholeness as well as the fullness of human experience. The discipleship expressed in the metaphor of the woman giving birth to a child in John 16.21–4 is appropriate here,[65] for the point is that the child will be born and that it will be received with joy.

For some, the process of reconstruction will be more difficult to accept than for others, but without some more comprehensive stripping of the set and some image-smashing of a radical kind as a preliminary to resetting the theological stage, it may well be that women's self-recovery will depend upon their refusal to bother any more with the Churches and their theology, in the confidence that 'means of grace' will be provided for them in some other way. Many women seem already to have made the decision to rely on themselves and whatever 'means of grace' are available to them, rather than on the institutions of Christianity, and how, if ever, those institutions can win their allegiance again in the near future is totally unclear to me.

For those who stay with Christianity, let me try to sum up in outline what I think is happening in Christian feminist theologizing. Women will not put up with any implication that there is a conflict between being female and feminine and godlikeness, (and femininity, like masculinity, may be an aspect of a person of either sex). They are especially sensitive to the incoherence between the proclamation of redemption-equivalence and gender models in doctrine and symbolism. They think that old stories can be retold and new ones invented to verbalize divine reality in a human manner which takes account of them and their experiences, and hopefully of neglected elements in men's lives too. They see that the language which mediates divine reality has differed, depending on its relationship to shifting contexts, and they want to imitate the motivation of those who have redeployed the language and perhaps even reuse some of the content. The point of it all is to try to get us to make an imaginative and moral shift, so that we can come to share a new vision of goodness and be given and gain access to it. The theological and ethical task that lies before them and other theologians is a massive one. We might also say that a poem by Emily Dickinson, written in 1862 and published in 1890, with the title 'Love's Baptism' represents the option which has now become clear to women, whether or not the task is completed well enough, and in time:

I'm ceded—I've stopped being Their's—
The name They dropped upon my face
With water, in the country church
Is finished using, now.
And They can put it with my Dolls,
My childhood, and the string of spools,
I've finished threading—too—

Baptized, before, without the choice,
But this time, consciously, of Grace!
Unto supremest name—
Called to my Full—The Crescent dropped—
Existence's whole Arc, filled up,
With one small Diadem.

My second Rank—too small the first—
Crowned—Crowing—on my Father's breast—
A half unconscious Queen—
But this time—Adequate—Erect,
With Will to choose, or to reject,
And I choose, just a Crown—[66]

Notes

1   Cady Stanton, *The Woman's Bible*, part 2, p. 114.
2   Ecumenical Society of the Blessed Virgin Mary (hereafter called ESBVM), *The Akathistos Hymn* (1987), p. 17.
3   Hilda Graef, *Mary: A History of Doctrine and Devotion* (Sheed & Ward 1985), p. 45, quoting from the twelfth-century Amadeus of Lausanne: '... The Holy Spirit will come upon you, that at his touch your womb may tremble and swell, your spirit rejoice and your womb flower...'
4   ibid., p. 176.
5   Marina Warner, *Alone of All her Sex: The Myth and Cult of the Virgin Mary* (Picador 1985), p. 43.
6   ibid., p. 57.
7   Stanton, *The Woman's Bible*, p. 31; see also Woolf, *Three Guineas*, pp. 183-4.

8 Mary Daly, *Beyond God the Father*, 1st pub. 1973 (Women's Press 1986), pp. 181f; *Gyn/Ecology*, 1st pub. 1978 (Women's Press 1984), pp. 83f; *Pure Lust* (Women's Press 1984), pp. 96f.

9 Daly, *Beyond God the Father*, p. 62.

10 Daly, *Pure Lust*, p. 128.

11 Bynum, 'Women Mystics and Eucharistic Devotion in the Thirteenth Century', p. 206.

12 Warner, *Alone of All her Sex*, p. 41.

13 Carol Delaney, 'The Meaning of Paternity and the Virgin Birth Debate' in *Man*, 21:3 (1986), pp. 454–513.

14 *The Akathistos Hymn*, p. 19.

15 ibid., p. 33.

16 John McHugh, 'The Virginal Conception of Jesus', paper of 25 October 1985, published for the ESBVM, p. 6.

17 Sarah Maitland, *Daughter of Jerusalem* (Pavanne 1987), p. 30.

18 Ruether, 'Misogynism and Virginal Feminism', p. 166.

19 Rosemary Radford Ruether, *Mary, the Feminine Face of the Church* (SCM Press 1979); also her *Sexism and God-talk: Towards a Feminist Theology* (SCM Press 1983), ch. 6.

20 Warner, *Alone of All her Sex*, 'The Hour of our Death', pp. 315–31.

21 ibid., p. 325.

22 Elisabeth Moltmann-Wendel, *A land Flowing with Milk and Honey*, tr. John Bowden (SCM Press 1986), pp. 193f.

23 Jill Robson, 'Mary: My Sister', in Furlong (ed.), *Feminine in the Church*, pp. 119–38.

24 Eric Doyle, 'God and the Feminine' in *Clergy Review*, 56 (1985), pp. 866–77, esp. p. 870.

25 Richard D. Kahoe, 'Social Science of Gender Differences: Ideological Battleground' in *Religious Studies Review*, 11:3 (1985), pp. 223–7.

26 ibid., p. 224.

27 H. Scott Holland, 'Faith' in *Lux Mundi*, p. 12.

28 ibid., p. 13.

29 Paget (ed.), *Henry Scott Holland*, pp. 121–2.

30 H. Scott Holland, 'Faith', p. 8.

31 ibid., p. 29.

32 ibid., p. 39.

33 Gerard Manley Hopkins, *Poems and prose*, ed. W. H. Gardner (Penguin 1953), p. 51.

34 Thomas H. Johnson (ed.), *The Poems of Emily Dickinson* (Cambridge, Mass, Harvard University Press, 1955), vol. 3, p. 1069.

35 Sylvia Plath, *Collected poems*, ed. Ted Hughes (Faber & Faber 1981), p. 179. See also Joyce Carol Oates, 'The Death Throes of Romanticism: The Poetry of Sylvia Plath' in *New Heaven, New Earth: The Visionary Experience in Literature* (New York, Vanguard, 1974), pp. 111–40.

36 Kari Elisabeth Børresen, 'God's Image, Man's Image? Female Metaphors describing God in the Christian Tradition' in *Temenos*, 19 (1983), pp. 17–32, esp. p. 29.

37 Alan E. Lewis (ed.), *The Motherhood of God* (St Andrew's Press 1984).

38   Phyllis Trible, *God and the Rhetoric of Sexuality* (Philadelphia, Fortress Press, 1978).

39   Gail Ramshaw Schmidt, 'Lutheran Liturgical Prayer and God as Mother' in *Worship*, 52:6 (1978), pp. 517–42.

40   Joan Chamberlain Engelsman, *The Feminine Dimension of the Divine* (Philadelphia, Westminster Press, 1979).

41   ibid., p. 144.

42   Børresen, 'God's Image', p. 23.

43   Aelred of Rievaulx quoted in Bynum, *Jesus as Mother*, p. 123.

44   See Sally Thompson, 'The Problem of the Cistercian Nuns' in Derek Baker (ed.), *Medieval Women*, pp. 227–52.

45   *The Prayers and Meditations of St Anselm*, tr. Sister Benedicta Ward (Penguin 1973), pp. 155–6.

46   Jasper Hopkins and Herbert W. Richardson (eds. and trs.), *Anselm of Canterbury* (SCM Press 1974), 1, p. 56.

47   Julian of Norwich, *Showings*, tr. E. Colledge and James Walsh (New York, Paulist Press, 1978), pp. 177–8.

48   ibid., pp. 207–8.

49   ibid., pp. 294. See also A. M. Allchin, 'Julian of Norwich and the Continuity of Tradition' in *Julian, Woman of our Day* (ed. Robert Llewelyn (Darton, Longman & Todd, 1985), pp. 27–40; J. H. P. Clark, 'Nature, Grace and the Trinity in Julian of Norwich' in *Downside Review* (July 1982), pp. 203–20.

50   Børresen, 'God's Image', p. 27.

51   Bynum, *Jesus as Mother*, p. 140.

52   Hans Urs von Balthasar, *Thérèse of Lisieux*, tr. D. Nicholl (Sheed & Ward 1953), pp. 75–7.

53   Margaret Hebblethwaite, *Motherhood and God* (Geoffrey Chapman 1984).

54   Taylor, *Eve and the New Jerusalem*, pp. 161–72.

55   Robley Edward Whitson (ed.), *The Shakers: Two Centuries of Spiritual Reflection* (SPCK 1983), pp. 3f.

56   ibid., p. 175. See also Ruether, *Womanguides*, pp. 33–4.

57   Cady Stanton, *The Woman's Bible*, p. 136.

58   A. Flew, 'Theology and Falsification', pp. 96–9 of A. Flew and A. MacIntyre (eds.), *New Essays in Philosophical Theology* (SCM Press 1955).

59   Luise Eichenbaum and Susie Orbach, *What Do Women Want?* (Fontana 1983).

60   Whitehouse, *The Authority of Grace*, p. 192.

61   Pohier, *God in Fragments*, p. 235.

62   Elisabeth Schüssler Fiorenza, 'Feminist Theology and New Testament Interpretation' in the *Journal for the Study of the Old Testament*, pp. 32–46, esp. p. 44; and see her collection, *Bread not Stone* (Boston, Mass., Beacon Press, 1984).

63   Elisabeth Schüssler Fiorenza, *In Memory of Her: A Feminist Theological Reconstruction of Christian Origins* (SCM Press 1983), p. 351.

64   Elisabeth Schüssler Fiorenza, 'The Sophia-God of Jesus and the Discipleship of Women', in Joann Wolski Conn (ed.), *Women's Spirituality:*

Resources for Christian Development (New York, Paulist Press, 1986), pp. 261–73; reprinted from *In Memory of Her* and placed in relation to a selection of other valuable material by a variety of authors from their different perspectives.

65   Francis J. Moloney, *Woman: First among the Faithful* (Darton, Longman & Todd, 1985), pp. 82–7; Frances Young, *Can these Dry Bones Live?* (SCM Press 1982), pp. 43–53.

66   Emily Dickinson, *The Poems*, ed. Johnson, vol. 2, pp. 389–90.

BIBLIOGRAPHY

Note: The place of publication is included only where this is outside the UK.

Anderson, Herbert, *The Family and Pastoral Care* (Philadelphia, Fortress Press, 1984).

Armstrong, Karen, *Beginning the World* (Pan Books 1983).

Armstrong, Karen, *The Gospel According to Woman* (Elm Tree Books 1986).

Armstrong, Karen, *Through the Narrow Gate* (Pan Books 1981).

Ascher, Carole, De Salvo, Louise and Ruddick, Sara (eds.), *Between Women* (Boston, Beacon Press, 1984).

Baade, James, 'Witness to the Cross' (*The Tablet*, 14 April 1984), pp. 335–57.

Baker, Derek (ed.), *Medieval Women* (Basil Blackwell 1978).

Balthasar, Hans Urs von, *Elizabeth of Dijon: An Interpretation of her Spiritual Mission*, tr. A. V. Littledale (Harvill Press 1956).

Balthasar, Hans Urs von, *Thérèse of Lisieux*, tr. D. Nichol (Sheed and Ward 1953).

Barrett, Michele (ed.), *Virginia Woolf: Women and Writing* (Women's Press 1979).

Bass, Dorothy C., 'Women's Studies and Biblical Studies: An Historical Perspective' (*Journal for the Study of the Old Testament*, 22, 1982), pp. 6–12.

Battin, M. Pabst and Mayo, D. J., *Suicide, the Philosophical Issues* (New York, St Martin's Press, 1980).

Beaumont, E., *The Theme of Beatrice in the Plays of Claudel* (Rockcliff 1954).

Beauvoir, Simone de, *The Second Sex*, tr. H. M. Parshley (Penguin 1984).

Bell, Quentin, *Virginia Woolf: 2. Mrs Woolf 1912–1941* (Hogarth Press 1972).

Bell, Rudolph M., *Holy Anorexia* (Chicago University Press 1985).

Børresen, Kari Elisabeth, 'God's Image, Man's Image? Female Metaphors Describing God in the Christian Tradition (*Temenos*, 19, 1983), pp. 17–32.

Børresen, Kari Elisabeth, 'Imago Dei, Privilège Masculin? Interprétation Augustinienne et Pseudo-Augustinienne de Gen. 1.27 et 1 Cor. 11.7' (*Augustinianum*, 25, 1985), pp. 213–34.

Børresen, Kari Elisabeth, *Subordination and Equivalence: The Nature and Role of Woman in Augustine and Thomas Aquinas*, tr. Charles H. Talbot (Washington DC, University Press of America 1981).

Boyd, Nancy, *Josephine Butler, Octavia Hill, Florence Nightingale: Three Victorian Women who Changed their World* (Macmillan 1982).

Brabazon, James, *Dorothy Sayers: The Life of a Courageous Woman* (Gollancz 1981).

Brett, Edward Tracy, *Humbert of the Romans: His Life and Views of Thirteenth Century Society* (Toronto, Pontifical Institute of Medieval Studies, 1984).

Bynum, Caroline Walker, *Jesus as Mother: Studies in the Spirituality of the High Middle Ages* (California University Press 1982).

Bynum, Caroline Walker, 'Woman Mystics and Eucharistic Devotion in the Thirteenth Century (*Women's Studies*, 11, 1984), pp. 179–214.

Cabaud, J., *Simone Weil: A Fellowship in Love* (Harvill Press 1964).

Callam, Daniel (tr.), St Ambrose on Virginity (Saskatoon, Peregrina, 1980).

Cameron, Rod (ed.), *The Other Gospels: Non-Canonical Gospel Texts* (Philadelphia, Westminster Press, 1982).

Chadwick, H., *Augustine* (Oxford University Press 1986).

Christ, Carol P. and Plaskow, Judith (eds.), *Womanspirit Rising* (New York, Harper and Row, 1979).

Clark, Elizabeth A., *Women in the Early Church*, Message of the Fathers of the Church, 13 (Wilmington, Denver, Michael Glazier, 1983).

Clark, J. H. P., 'Nature, Grace and the Trinity in Julian of Norwich' (*Downside Review*, July 1982), pp. 203–20.

Claudel, P., *L'Annonce faite à Marie* (Paris, Gallimard, 1940).

Conn, Joann Wolski (ed.), *Women's Spirituality: Resources for Christian Development* (New York, Paulist Press, 1986).

Corrigan, Dame Felicitas (ed.), *Helen Waddell: A Biography* (Gollancz 1986).

Corrigan, Dame Felicitas (ed.), *More Latin Lyrics from Virgil to Milton* tr. Helen Waddell (Gollancz 1976).

Cross, Amanda, *Death in a Tenured Position* (New York, Ballantine, 1981).

Daly, Mary, *Beyond God the Father* 1st pub. 1973 (Women's Press 1985).

Daly, Mary, *Gyn/Ecology*, 1st pub. 1978 (Women's Press 1984).

Daly, Mary, *Pure Lust* (Women's Press 1984).

Daly, Mary, 'The Women's Movement: An Exodus Community' (*Religious Education*, 67:5, 1972), pp. 327–34.

Daube, David, 'The Linguistics of Suicide' (*Philosophy and Public Affairs*, 1:4, 1972), pp. 367–437.

Delaney, Carol, 'The Meaning of Paternity and the Virgin Birth Debate' (*Man*, 21:3, 1986), pp. 454–513.

Doyle, Eric, 'God and the Feminine' (*Clergy Review*, 56, 1985), pp. 866–77.

Dronke, Peter, *Women Writers of the Middle Ages* (Cambridge University Press 1984).

Ecumenical Society of the Blessed Virgin Mary, *The Akathistos Hymn* (ESBVM 1987).

Egerton, George, *Keynotes and Discords* (Virago 1983).

Eichenbaum, Luise and Orbach, Susie, *What do Women Want?* (Fontana 1983).

Ellsberg, Robert (ed.), *By Little and by Little: The Selected Writings of Dorothy Day* (New York, Borzoi, 1983).

Engelsman, Joan Chamberlain, *The Feminine Dimension of the Divine* (Philadelphia, Westminster Press, 1979).

Evans, Mary, *Woman in the Bible* (Paternoster Press 1983).

Fell, Margaret, *Women's speaking justified, proved and allowed of by the Scriptures, all such as speak by the spirit and power of the Lord Jesus. And how women were the first that preached the tidings of the resurrection of Jesus, and were sent by Christ's own command, before he ascended to the Father, John 20.17*, 1st pub. 1666 (Amherst, Mass., for the Mosher Book and Tract Committee, New England Yearly Meetings of Friends, 1980).

Fiorenza, Elisabeth Schüssler, *Bread not Stone* (Boston, Beacon Press, 1984).

Fiorenza, Elisabeth Schüssler, 'Feminist Theology and New Testament Interpretation (*Journal for the Study of the Old Testament*, 22, 1982), pp. 32–46.

Fiorenza, Elisabeth Schüssler, *In Memory of Her: A Feminist Theological Reconstruction of Christian Origins* (SCM Press 1983).

Fiorenza, Elisabeth Schüssler and Collins, Mary (eds.), *Women-Invisible in Theology and Church* (T. and T. Clark 1985).

107

First, Ruth and Scott, Ann, *Olive Schreiner* (Andre Deutsch 1980).

Flew, A. and MacIntyre, A. (eds.), *New Essays in Philosophical Theology* (SCM Press 1955).

Forster, E. M., *A Room with a View* (Penguin 1986).

Forster, Margaret, *Significant Sisters: The Grass Roots of Active Feminism, 1839–1939 (Penguin 1984).*

France, Anatole, Thaïs, tr. Robert B. Douglas (John Lane 1928).

Furlong, Monica (ed.), *Feminine in the Church* (SPCK 1984).

Gordon, Lyndall, *Virginia Woolf: A Writer's Life* (Oxford University Press 1984).

Gore, Charles (ed.), *Lux Mundi: A Series of Studies in the Religion of the Incarnation* (John Murray 1904).

Graef, Hilda, *Mary: A History of Doctrine and Devotion* (Sheed and Ward 1985).

Griffin, Elisabeth, *In Her Own Right: The Life of Elizabeth Cady Stanton* (Oxford University Press 1984).

Hannay, Margaret P., '"Through the World like a Flame": Christology in the dramas of Dorothy L. Sayers' (*Vox Benedictina*, 2:2, 1985), pp. 148–66.

Hayter, Mary, *The New Eve in Christ* (SPCK 1987).

Hebblethwaite, Margaret, *Motherhood and God* (Geoffrey Chapman 1984).

Hillesum, Etty, *An Interrupted Life: The Diaries of Etty Hillesum, 1941–1943* (New York, Pocket Books, 1985).

Hogg, J. T., 'Mount Grace Charterhouse and Late Medieval English Spirituality' (*Analecta Cartusiana*, 1980) pp. 1–43.

Holland, Henry Scott, *A Bundle of Memories* (Wells, Gardner, Darton and Co. 1915).

Holland, Henry Scott, *Fibres of Faith* (Wells, Gardner, Darton and Co. 1910).

Holland, Henry Scott, *Our Neighbours: A Handbook for the C.S.U.* (Mowbray 1911).

Hooker, Morna D., 'Authority on her Head: An Examination of 1 Cor. 11.10' (*New Testament Studies*, 10, 1963–4).

Hopkins, Gerard Manley, *Poems and Prose*, ed. H. W. Gardner (Penguin 1953).

Hopkins, Jasper, and Richardson, Herbert W. (eds. and trs.), *Anselm of Canterbury* (SCM Press 1974), p. 1.

IBVM (ed.), *The Heart and Mind of Mary Ward* (Anthony Clarke 1985).

Johnson, Thomas H. (ed.), *The Poems of Emily Dickinson* (Cambridge, Mass., Harvard University Press, 1955), p. 3.

Julian of Norwich, *Showings*, tr. E. Colledge and James Walsh (New York, Paulist Press and London, SPCK, 1978).

Kahoe, Richard D., 'Social Science of Gender Differences: Ideological Battleground' (*Religious Studies Review*, 11:3, 1985), pp. 223–7.

Kant, Immanuel, *Critique of Practical Reason* etc., tr. T. K. Abbott (Longman 1967).

Kant, Immanuel, *Religion Within the Limits of Reason Alone*, trs. T. M. Greene and H. H. Hudson (New York, Harper and Row, 1960).

Kempe, Margery, *The Book of Margery Kempe*, tr. B. A. Windeatt (Penguin 1985).

King, Helen, 'Sacrificial Blood: The Role of the Amnion in Ancient Gynecology' (*Helios*, Women in Antiquity special issue, 13:2, 1986.

Köhler, Mathilde, *Maria Ward: ein Frauenschicksal des 17. Jarhhunderts* (Munich, Köset-Verlag, 1984).

Kraemer, Ross S., 'The Conversion of Women to Ascetic Forms of Christianity' (*Signs*, 16:2, 1980), pp. 298–307.

Kraemer, Ross S., 'Women in the Religions of the Graeco-Roman World' (*Religious Studies Review*, 9:2, April 1983).

Krige, Uys, *Olive Schreiner: A Selection* (Oxford University Press 1986).

Labalme, Patricia H. (ed.), *Beyond their Sex: Learned Women of the European Past* (New York University Press 1980).

LaPorte, Jean, *The Role of Women in Early Christianity*, Studies in Women and Religion 7 (New York, Edwin Mellen Press, 1982).

Leach, William, *True Love and Perfect Union: The Feminist Reform of Sex and Society* (Routledge and Kegan Paul 1981).

Leclerq, Jean, *The Love of Learning and the Desire for God*, tr. Catherine Misrahi (New York, Fordham University Press, 1974).

Leloir, Louis, 'Woman and the Desert Fathers' (*Vox Benedictina*, 3:3, 1986), pp. 207–27.

Lessing, Doris, *The Golden Notebook* (Granada 1981).

Lewis, Alan E. (ed.), *The Motherhood of God* (St Andrew's Press 1984).

Littlehales, Margaret Mary, *Mary Ward: A Woman for all Seasons* (Catholic Truth Society 1982).

Llewelyn, Robert (ed.), *Julian, Woman of our Day* (Darton, Longman and Todd 1985).

Lubac, Henri de, *The Motherhood of the Church*, tr. Sr Sergia Englund (San Francisco, Ignatius Press, 1982).

MacKinnon, D. M., *Explorations in Theology*, 5 (SCM Press 1979).

Maitland, Sarah, *Daughter of Jerusalem* (Pavanne 1987).

Marcus, Jane (ed.), *New Feminist Essays on Virginia Woolf* (Macmillan 1981).

Martimort, Aimé Georges, *Deaconesses: An Historical Study*, tr. K. D. Whitehead (San Francisco, Ignatius Press, 1986).

Mathews, Donald G., 'Women's History/Everyone's History' (*Quarterly Review*, 1:5, 1981), pp. 41–60.

McHugh, John, 'The Virginal Conception of Jesus', paper of 25 October 1985, pub. for the ESBVM.

Midgley, Mary, 'Sex and Personal Identity' (*Encounter*, June 1984) pp. 50–5.

Midgley, Mary, and Hughes, Judith, *Women's Choices: Philosophical Problems facing Feminism* (Weidenfeld and Nicolson 1983).

Miller, William D., *Dorothy Day: A Biography* (New York, Harper and Row, 1982).

Moloney, Francis J., *Woman: First among the Faithful* (Darton, Longman and Todd 1985).

Moltmann-Wendel, Elisabeth, *A Land Flowing with Milk and Honey*, tr. John Bowden (SCM Press 1986).

Moltmann-Wendel, Elisabeth, *The Women around Jesus*, tr. J. Bowden (SCM Press 1986).

Mounteer, Carl A., 'Guilt, Martyrdom and Monasticism' (*Journal of Psychohistory*, 9:2, 1981), pp. 145–71.

Murdoch, Iris, *Henry and Cato* (Penguin 1983).

Oates, Joyce Carol, *New Heaven, New Earth: The Visionary Experience in Literature* (New York, Vanguard Press, 1974).

Oates, Joyce Carol, *The Profane Art: Essays and Reviews* (New York, E. P. Dutton, 1983).

Obelkevich, Jim, Roper, Lyndal, and Samuel, Raphael (eds.), *Disciplines of Faith: Studies in Religion, Politics and Patriarchy* (Routledge and Kegan Paul 1987).

O'Faolain, Julia, and Martines, Lauro (eds.), *Not in God's Image* (New York, Harper and Row, 1973).

O'Flaherty, K., *Paul Claudel and 'The Tidings Brought to Mary'* (Basil Blackwell 1948).

Oppenheimer, Helen, 'Christian Flourishing' (*Religious Studies*, 5, 1969), pp. 163–71.

Oppenheimer, Helen, 'Life after Death' (*Theology*, 82, 1979), pp. 328–35.

Paget, Stephen (ed.), *Henry Scott Holland: Memoir and Letters* (John Murray 1921).

Pargeter, Edith, *The Heaven Tree*, trilogy, 1 (Macdonald 1986).

Pétrement, Simone, *Simone Weil: A Life*, tr. R. Rosenthal (Mowbray 1976).

Petroff, Elizabeth Alvida (ed.), *Medieval Women's Visionary Literature* (Oxford University Press 1985).

Phillips, Ann (ed.), *A Newnham Anthology* (Cambridge University Press 1979).

Plath, Sylvia, *Ariel* (Faber and Faber 1965).

Plath, Sylvia, *Collected Poems* (ed. Ted Hughes (Faber and Faber 1981).

Pohier, Jacques, *God in Fragments*, tr. John Bowden (SCM Press 1985).

Poole, Roger, *The Unknown Virginia Woolf* (Harvester Press 1982).

Raitt, Jill, 'The *Vagina Dentata* and the *Immaculatus Uterus Divini Fontis*' (*Journal of the American Academy of Religion*, 48, September 1980), pp. 415–31.

Reardon, B. M. G. (ed.), *Henry Scott Holland: A Selection from his Writings* (SPCK 1962).

Rich, Adrienne, *A Wild Patience has Taken Me this Far* (New York, W. W. Norton, 1981).

Ruether, Rosemary Radford, *Mary, the Feminine Face of the Church* (SCM Press 1979).

Ruether, Rosemary Radford, *Sexism and God-Talk: Towards a Feminist Theology* (SCM Press 1983).

Ruether, Rosemary Radford (ed.), *Religion and Sexism: Images of Woman in the Jewish and Christian Traditions* (New York, Simon and Schuster, 1974).

Ruether, Rosemary Radford (ed.), *Womanguides: Readings Towards a Feminist Theology* (Boston, Beacon Press, 1985).

Russell, Letty M. (ed.), *Feminist Interpretation of the Bible* (Basil Blackwell 1985).

Sayers, Dorothy L., *Creed or Chaos and Other Essays in Popular Theology* (Methuen 1945).

Sayers, Dorothy L., *Further Papers on Dante* (Methuen 1957).

Sayers, Dorothy L. *The Man Born to be King* (Gollancz 1943).

Sayers, Dorothy L., *Unpopular Opinions* (Gollancz 1946).

Schmidt, Gail Ramshaw, 'Lutheran Liturgical Prayer and God as Mother' (*Worship*, 52:6, 1978), pp. 517-42.

Schreiner, Olive, *The Story of an African Farm* (Penguin 1982).

Slee, Nicola, 'Parables and Women's Experience' (*Modern Churchman*, 26:2, 1984), pp. 20-31.

Sophocles, *The Theban plays*, tr. E. F. Watling (Penguin 1974).

Spender, Dale, *Feminist Theories* (Women's Press 1983).

Springstead, Eric O., *Simone Weil and the Suffering of Love* (Cambridge, Mass., Cowley, 1986).

Stacpoole, Alberic, 'The Making of a Monastic Historian 2' (*The Ampleforth Journal*, 80:2, 1975), pp. 19-38.

Stanton, Elizabeth Cady, *The Woman's Bible* (Polygon 1985).

Steiner, George, *Antigones: The Antigone Myth in Western Literature, Art and Culture* (Clarendon Press 1986).

Stewart, Columba, 'The Portrayal of Women in the Sayings and Stories of the Desert' (*Vox Benedictina*, 2:1, 1985), pp. 5-23.

Stewart, Columba (tr.), *The World of the Desert Fathers* (SLG Press 1986).

Stubbs, Patricia, *Woman and Fiction: Feminism and the Novel, 1880-1920* (Methuen 1979).

The Tablet 'Notebook' (26 January 1985).

Taylor, Barbara, *Eve and the New Jerusalem: Socialism and Feminism in the Nineteenth Century* (Virago 1984).

Thurman, Judith, *Isak Dinesen: The Life of Karen Blixen* (Penguin 1982).

Trible, Phyllis, 'Biblical Theology as Women's Work' (*Religion in Life*, 44, 1975), pp. 7-13.

Trible, Phyllis, *God and the Rhetoric of Sexuality* (Philadelphia, Fortress Press, 1978).

Trible, Phyllis, *Texts of Terror: Literary Feminist Readings of Biblical Narratives* (Philadelphia, Fortress Press, 1984).

Tugwell, Simon, *Ways of Imperfection: An Exploration of Christian Spirituality* (Darton, Longman and Todd 1984).

Waddell, Helen, *Beasts and Saints* (Constable 1942).

Waddell, Helen, *The Desert Fathers* (Constable 1954).

Waddell, Helen, *The Wandering Scholars* (Penguin 1954).

Ward, Sister Benedicta (tr.), The Prayers and Meditations of St Anselm (Penguin 1973).

Warner, Marina, *Alone of all her Sex: The Myth and Cult of the Virgin Mary* (Picador 1985).

Warnicke, Retha M., *Women of the English Renaissance and Reformation* (Greenwood Press 1983).

The Way Supplement 'Mary Ward: Essays in Honour of the Fourth Centenary of her Birth' (53, 1985).

Weil, Simone, *First and Last Notebooks*, tr. R. Rees (Oxford University Press 1970).

Weil, Simone, *Intimations of Christianity among the Greeks*, tr. E. C. Geissbuhler (Routledge and Kegan Paul 1976).

Weil, Simone, *The Need for Roots*, tr. A. F. Wills (Routledge and Kegan Paul 1978).

Weil, Simone, *The Notebooks*, 2 vols, tr. A. Wills (Routledge and Kegan Paul 1976).

Weil, Simone, *Seventy Letters*, tr. R. Rees (Oxford University Press 1965).

Weil, Simone, *Waiting on God*, tr. E. Crauford (Fontana 1974).

Whigham-Price, A., *The Ladies of Castlebrae* (Sutton 1985).

White, Antonia, *Frost in May* (Fontana/Virago 1982).

Whitehouse, W. A., *The Authority of Grace* (T. and T. Clark 1981).

Whitson, Robley Edward (ed.), *The Shakers: Two Centuries of Spiritual Reflection* (SPCK 1983).

Wilson, Katharina M. (ed.), *Medieval Women Writers* (Athens, Georgia University Press, 1984).

Wilson, Katharina M. (tr.), *The Dramas of Hrotsvit of Gandersheim* (Saskatoon, Matrologia Latina and Peregrina Publishing, 1985).

Witherington, Ben III, *Women in the Ministry of Jesus: A Study of Jesus' Attitudes to Women and their Roles as Reflected in his Earthly Life* (Cambridge University Press 1984).

Woodbridge, Linda, *Women and the English Renaissance: Literature and the Nature of Womankind, 1540–1620* (Harvester Press 1984).

Woolf, Rosemary, *The English Religious Lyric in the Middle Ages* (Oxford University Press 1968).

Woolf, Virginia, *A Room of One's Own*, 1st pub. 1929 (Panther 1985).

Woolf, Virginia, *Three Guineas*, 1st pub. 1938 (Hogarth Press 1986).

Woolf, Virginia, *The Years*, 1st pub. 1937 (Granada 1982).

Young, Francis, *Can these Dry Bones Live?* (SCM Press 1982).
Ziegler, Joanna, 'Women of the Middle Ages: Some Questions Regarding the Béguines and Devotional Art' (*Vox Benedictina*, 3:4, 1986), pp. 338–57:

INDEX

115